Sons at War

Sons at War

THE TRUE STORY OF TWO YOUNG MEN DESTINED FROM BIRTH TO COLLIDE IN DEATH

———

Jane Sweetland

ISBN-13: 9781542617659
ISBN-10: 1542617650
Library of Congress Control Number: 2017900763
CreateSpace Independent Publishing Platform
North Charleston, South Carolina

Dedicated to the families of
Ted Sweetland
and
Joachim Müncheberg

Contents

Prologue · ix

Part One: Born into Privilege 1918 – 1932 · · · · · · · · · · · · · · · · · · 1
Chapter 1   In the Beginning · 3
Chapter 2   Born Lucky · 9
Chapter 3   Children at Play · 16

Part Two: Coming of Age 1933-1937 · 23
Chapter 4   Divided Societies · 25
Chapter 5   The Year that Changed Everything · · · · · · · · · · · · · · · · 31
Chapter 6   Belonging · 44
Chapter 7   The Olympics Showcase the Reich · · · · · · · · · · · · · · · · 49
Chapter 8   Diverging Roads · 53

Part Three: Worlds Apart 1938 – 1940 · · · · · · · · · · · · · · · · · · · 57
Chapter 9   The Third Reich Expands · 59
Chapter 10 The Time Has Come ... · 72
Chapter 11 Fight or Flight · 84

Part Four: Worlds Collide 1941 – 1943 · · · · · · · · · · · · · · · · · · · 101
Chapter 12 From the Pacific to the Mediterranean · · · · · · · · · · · · · 103
Chapter 13 The Balance Begins to Tip · 117
Chapter 14 In the Air Stars Cross · 141

Epilogue · 159
Acknowledgements · 169
Bibliography · 173
End Notes · 179

Prologue

———

THE DAY HE BEGAN HIS war diary, Ted Sweetland was in the Army Air Corps, stationed at Luke Air Force Base in Arizona. The first entry is dated December 7, 1941. The cloth cover is faded blue and the writing is round and firm.

> *Carla and I were sitting in the car drinking beer and arguing the universality or personalization of truth, beauty, and morality, when some citizen came up to the car and asked if we had been listening to the radio. We had not. He informed us that Japan had bombed Manila and Honolulu. She was shocked; I elated: the cards are all on the table and may the devil take the hindmost (of which there are many). Isn't it marvelous that with social stability what it is that such violent upheavals can still result! I proposed a toast that it be long and bloody but contritely added "for those that deserve it" (also of which there are many).*

The diary is short, like my Uncle Ted's service. The last entry, on page sixty, is dated March 13, 1943, ten days before he was shot down over North Africa. His body was never recovered, and as far as I could tell, no one in the family knew the name of the German who killed him. But seventy years after World War II ended, it wasn't hard for me to find a name.

The man who killed my father's brother was Joachim Müncheberg. He was born just six months before Ted and when I saw his picture I thought they looked a little like cousins with their smooth white faces, light hair and deep blue eyes. Their smiles are framed with parentheses and form a contented ledge above determined chins.

Ted Sweetland
June 27, 1919 – March 23, 1943

Joachim Müncheberg
December 31, 1918 – March 23, 1943

They weren't cousins though; they were enemies in a war in which 27,600 people died every day. My uncle was just one of the three hundred American soldiers whose destiny was to join those who fell on that blue sky morning. Most rivals who died in WWII were anonymous to each other except in a general sense: the abstract enemy. I had found the name of the man who killed my uncle; I had even found a biography, a eulogy that commemorated his military history, but there wasn't much about him before he joined the Wehrmacht, and Joachim was not born a fighter pilot any more than Ted was.

I wondered who they had been before they were warriors. What games did they play when they were children? Had they always wanted to fly? What did they learn at home? In school? In church? What had they learned to believe? What had they been taught to ignore?

I never knew my uncle, but I had mosaic pieces of his life: a boy who asked Santa for a puppy, a harmonica and a toy cannon that could shoot cherry bombs. A young man who went to a Jesuit high school in California, debated the efficacy of America's neutrality position, met Pope Pius XI in 1938, and dropped out of college to enlist in the Army Air Corps. Until the day she died, his mother kept the letter he wrote from Fort Dix, New Jersey, before he shipped out to England. The light blue airmail paper is thin, worn from age and reading. It's dated September 1, 1942.

> *Mother, I love you as I never shall another woman because I know your love for me is without thought of yourself. It is wonderful to know a person could care that much for another — born with pain, reared with trouble, and separated with sorrow, a thankless job!*
>
> *Dad, I admire you more than I can say. Your devotion and guidance have been so much help to me that I will never be able to sufficiently thank you. I will endeavor not to make it in vain.*

Ted's life was destined to end just shy of his twenty-fourth birthday. He was flying "tail end Charlie" with the 5th squadron when Joachim, the commander of the German squadron, Jagdgeschwader 77, singled him out of the formation and sent him spiraling to earth.

It was an unfair fight, really. Ted was an American rookie, deployed in the fall of 1942, to England where he learned to fly the feisty little English fighter: The Spitfire. Capable of flying low and fast, the Spitfire had a single pilot, strapped into the cockpit. Since 1939, Joachim had been flying its German counterpart, a small lethal fighting machine: The Messerschmitt. Ted was on his tenth combat sortie, while Joachim, a seasoned professional, was on his 500th mission. Joachim's plane was easy to identify, with its red heart emblazoned on the fuselage and dozens of black painted tick marks feathering the tail like plumage, one for every enemy shot down.

Joachim's war started when Germany attacked Poland on September 1, 1939, long before the Americans joined. In the fall of 1939, while Joachim was patrolling the English Channel, Ted was in college, writing a column, often satirical, for the school newspaper. In response to Hitler's bombastic speech on October 6, 1939, Ted wrote a series of clipped observations. He was watching and listening, but the war was a story being played out on a stage six thousand miles away from his room with a view of an American college campus where boys sat in groups on wide lawns and meandered to class on graveled paths.

> *Hitler gave a cute speech in Berlin last week. There's a rumor that he is going to take up fireside chatting. …*
>
> *Will the combatants be able to refrain from using poison gases? Hitler wants to, it is a tempting weapon when things are looking bad. …*
>
> *In World War I, the United States was asked to sit in on a high-powered poker game (maybe we were trying to work our way through college) …Wilson went over with 14 points and was lucky to come home in a barrel.*

For Ted, World War I was a history lesson. It had happened before he was born half a world away and no one in his family had fought in it. For Joachim, the war was family history. His father had nearly died on the western front, and for Germany, the war ended badly: The German Empire including the Kingdom of Prussia was no more.

By 1936, while Ted was completing high school, Joachim was already serving in the Wehrmacht. In 1937, while Ted was a freshman in college, discussing philosophical questions under the shade of oaks trees on his campus near San Francisco, Joachim was in the air over Dresden learning to fly, and studying the physics of weapons and bullet trajectories.

Joachim would be a star student; he would become an Ace pilot and the Third Reich's propaganda machine would celebrate him as a hero. Postcards were made of him smiling from the cockpit—the young, handsome face of a terrible war initiated by a racist. Joachim would come to be known as "the Spitfire hunter" but he hadn't been born a hunter; like Ted, he was born someone's son.

I wanted to find his family, but time was not on my side. I knew he had died without having children of his own. Ted had six siblings, but they were all gone; Joachim had just one sister, Eva-Brigitte, born in 1917. If she lived through the war, she would have been twenty-seven in May 1945, when the Russians marched across Western Prussia, raping, burning, killing, and taking the spoils of war on their way to victory in Berlin. Most Germans in the area did not survive.

If she had married, she likely had taken her husband's name, so at first I thought Joachim was the end of the Müncheberg line. Then I discovered that in 1943, a decree to preserve surnames was enacted in Germany, inspired by the loss of a generation of young men like Joachim. If Eva-Brigitte Müncheberg had had children, she might have legally passed both her maiden and married names on to her children. I began combing footnotes of the books that included stories about Joachim and there I found her: Eva Hoffstätter-Müncheberg. Not long later, I found her youngest son, Christian Hoffstätter-Müncheberg.

I had no idea how Christian would receive my request to meet him, but I knew one thing: he had kept his mother's maiden name, a clearly traceable link to a warrior who had been a national hero during the Third Reich. My email was brief:

Hello Christian,
I am so pleased to have found you and I hope to be able to meet you... In very brief summary, your Uncle Joachim and my Uncle Ted were responsible for each other's deaths. While your uncle was an Ace, mine was a rookie, but both young men were intelligent, athletic, and beloved by colleagues. They were both men of honor.

I am writing about these two young men who fought on different sides in the war, but if they had been neighbors I believe they would have been friends. Born just six months apart, they would have shared their love of sports, music, and dogs. I think, too, they would have talked about life and what it means to be honorable. ...

Moments after I sent the email, I knew it was wrong. The bare truth was: our uncles had killed each other. Did I really believe they would have been friends? If they went to the same schools, would they have fought side by side for Hitler? For Roosevelt? If Ted had been born in Germany, would he have been a Nazi?

I knew that not all Germans were Nazis, but Joachim was highly decorated, clearly an enthusiastic fighter. Was he a Nazi? Did he believe that the war he was fighting was just? How could his nephews possibly welcome such questions?

It was a long three days before I heard from Christian.

Hallo Jane,
What a surprise receiving an email of a family member of a former "enemy" of Joachim, particularly that one of his last air fight! Most of us didn't even know Ted's name. We have no letters, no diary etc. of Joachim, only pictures in a private photo-album....

We exchanged several emails and arranged to meet a few weeks later, an interval that gave me time to visit Friedrichshof, where Joachim was born. I hoped the land would tell me something. I wanted to see where he had played as a boy. I wanted to imagine what he could see from his window.

———

In 1870, a year before the German Empire was established by Bismarck, the Pomeranian region was part of the Kingdom of Prussia, and that is where Joachim's grandfather, Hermann Müncheberg, purchased farmland. At the turn of the century the land, which had become part of the German Empire, was given to Joachim's father, Paul, who built a manor house in 1905, and sowed the fields with the soft greens of barley, clover, rye, potatoes, and oats. More than a century later, on the day I visited, the rolling fields undulated with brilliant yellow blooms of rapeseed.

At the end of the First World War when the German Empire collapsed, the Pomeranian region became part of the Weimar Republic and after World War II, the Treaty of Versailles gave substantial parts of what had been Germany's eastern districts to Poland. German citizens, including the Müncheberg family, were forced to leave, place names were changed and maps were redrawn, but the landscape today remains what it always was. There are no mountains, only low gently rolling fields as far as the eye can see until the horizon bends with the earth's curve. It was easy to imagine tanks crawling effortlessly across Joachim's family farm in the dry months or mired in mud during the spring thaw. When Joachim was a boy, there was an airstrip seven kilometers down the dusty road. From the upstairs window he would have seen metal birds bearing a solo pilot rumbling down the runway to take off or gliding in for a landing. But on the days I visited Friedrichshof, it was quiet, utterly and completely quiet, just the way it was on the last day of 1918, when Joachim was born, tiny and perfect.

I left Friedrichshof and took the train across Germany, through Dresden, Nuremburg and Cologne to meet Christian. I was nervous, but as he walked across the hotel lobby, his smile was welcoming. We spent several hours sharing stories about our uncles whose disparate, but eerily similar lives were destined to intersect in the air over Tunisia.

Later, at his home, we pored over piles of photographs and Joachim's personal photo album. Its brown leather cover shows the wear of its journey; it's one of the few belongings that survived his parents' flight before the Russians. The pages are black, and beneath each picture in white ink, Joachim has recorded his own history. On the first page is a picture of him, a tiny newborn bundle, nestled in his mother's arms. I had found the beginning.

Part One:
Born into Privilege 1918 – 1932

———

CHAPTER 1

In the Beginning

——

JOACHIM

ON THE LAST DAY OF December 1918, snow blanketed the rolling fields at Friedrichshof and the pond in front of the Müncheberg estate was frozen hard, but the two-story house Joachim's father, Paul Müncheberg, had built was warm. It was morning on New Year's Eve and the rich aroma of fresh bread baking rose to the bedroom upstairs where Erika was in labor, her mother at her shoulder and the midwife whispering encouragement. As the winter sunlight crept over the frozen earth, snow glittered and the Christmas tree laden with tinsel and glass ornaments dappled the rug with rainbow prisms. At 9:15 in the morning of December 31, 1918, Joachim was born. It was what Germans call "Sylvester Day," a day to celebrate endings and beginnings.[1]

By evening the fire roared in the great room downstairs where the family gathered: Paul's parents, Hermann and Louise, from their nearby farm at Schönfeld; Erika's parents, Karl and Emmy Ulrich, who had traveled nearly four hundred kilometers from Lubán in Upper Silesia to celebrate the holidays with their daughter's family. They may have feasted on one of the family's traditional favorites: codfish filets with a mustard-cream sauce and white wine. Joachim's older sister, eighteen-month-old Eva-Brigitte, was all dressed up for the occasion, feeling the excitement of the adults toasting the New Year. Erika was tired, but she had bathed and rested and wanted to join the evening festivities. She had the seat of honor near the fire, holding her precious bundle swaddled in white close against the warmth of her body. The year had begun with a blessing on the last day of 1918: the birth of a healthy son in a world that was, with the signing of the Armistice six weeks earlier, at peace. At midnight, a tray of doughnuts was passed around and everyone pondered their choice as hidden among the sweet pastry was one doughnut filled with mustard. That was the one that would bring luck for the year.

TED

Six months after Joachim was born, the day after the Treaty of Versailles officially ended WWI, Nell Reilly Sweetland went into labor with her fifth child. Ernest drove her to the hospital, not far from their spacious home in Montclair, New Jersey. Summer sun poured through high windows and made the white walls seem to shimmer as young nurses wearing crisp, white uniforms and crowned with starched caps moved quietly from bed to bed.[2] Nell had been a nurse herself and was familiar with the rituals of birth: the pain, the bustle, the crescendo and denouement when it would be revealed if she had been laboring for a son or a daughter.

It was a warm day, but not humid, and the new baby's four older siblings, Kathryn (10), Ruth (7); Jack (5) and Billy (3) were home, supervised by their nanny as they played in the backyard. Ernest waited in the lobby with the other men, some pacing, others smoking, glancing anxiously at the double doors that would swing open periodically. Ernest chose a corner seat and focused on the blue cloth-covered notebook in his lap, sketching, puzzling over the details of an idea he had: a device for filtering motor oil that could be used in automobiles. He already had over two dozen patents for large industrial filters, but this one was different. This one was a small filter; one for every car on the road. He thought cars would be the wave of the future, but oil was costly and it had to be dumped and replaced with fresh oil every two or three hundred miles. Ernest thought that filtering the oil while the car was running would keep the oil cleaner and save motorists the expense and trouble of having to change it so often. If it worked, it would be an idea worth millions.[3]

Thinking about the work in front of him made the wait easier. Nell was older, he knew, she had just turned thirty-nine, but there was no cause to worry. The other babies had not given her any trouble and this pregnancy had been like the others, easy. At least, he thought, she never complained.

At dusk, Ernest was called in to meet his third son. Nell was exhausted, but sitting up holding Theodore Reilly Sweetland, clean and swaddled, in her arms. On his way home to tell the others, Ernest sent a telegram to the Sweetland family in Carson City, Nevada and another to the Reilly family in Ireland. He used as few precious words as possible to send trans-Atlantic news that John and Catherine Reilly had a healthy grandson, Theodore Reilly Sweetland, who carried their family name. There would, Ernest knew, be drinks on the house at P. & E. Reilly's, Nell's family's pub on Main Street in Carrigallen.

The next day, Nell came home and was served tea in her room, along with the Evening Public Ledger, where the headline blared: *Treaty of Peace signed with Germany; Teutons Bow, Formally Closing War; Wilson Asks for Ratification of Pact.*

The story of the treaty with the Germans, variously called "Teutons" or "Huns" after fourth century warrior tribes, led in daily papers around the world as representatives from twenty-one countries gathered in the Hall of Mirrors in Versailles to formally end the war that had devastated a continent. Over forty-two million men had fought; more than half were killed, wounded, imprisoned or missing. Germany had been allowed little input as the victors crafted their terms and the two German delegates, who were little known bureaucrats, knew they were signing a document that humiliated their homeland. They signed under protest with pens they would throw away. A member of the British Delegation, Sir Harold Nicolson, commemorated the moment:

> *"We enter the Galerie des Glaces (Hall of Mirrors). It is divided into three sections. At the far end are the Press already thickly installed. In the middle there is a horse-shoe table for the plenipotentiaries. In front of that, like a guillotine, is the table for the signatures. It is supposed to be raised on a dais but, if so, the dais can be but a few inches high...There must be seats for over a thousand persons. This robs the ceremony of all privilege and therefore of all dignity.*
>
> *...the delegates arrive in little bunches and push up the central aisle slowly. Wilson and Lloyd George are among the last. They take their seats at the central table. The table is at last full. Clemenceau glances to right and left.*

...Through the door at the end appear two huissiers with silver chairs. They march in single file. After them come four officers of France, Great Britain, America and Italy. And then, isolated and pitiable, come the two German delegates. Dr. Muller, Dr. Bell. The silence is terrifying. Their feet upon a strip of parquet between the savonnerie carpets echo hollow and duplicate. They keep their eyes fixed away from those two thousand staring eyes, fixed upon the ceiling. They are deathly pale. They do not appear as representatives of a brutal militarism. The one is thick and pink-eye-lidded. The other is moonfaced and suffering.[4]

The Treaty of Versailles ensured that the aggressors would be punished: Germany was stripped of its colonies, boundaries were redrawn, land was expropriated on both fronts and a "Polish Corridor" cut East Prussia off from West Prussia. Germany's armed services were reduced and the country was forced to accept responsibility and liability for losses and damages of the Allies. A strict, and impossible schedule of reparations insured that the people would continue to suffer deprivation as food, coal, and heating oil were shipped across the border to their former enemies. The German people would be hungry and humiliated and they would not forget.

The United States Congress was dominated by Republicans who never ratified the treaty as it included President Wilson's idea that a League of Nations should be established. The League's charge would be to preserve world peace and this, Congress and many Americans believed, would force the United States into foreign wars. Ted's father likely sided with the Republicans, but Nell prayed for peace and mourned the boys who gave their lives. Officially, soldiers had to be 19 years old, but many were younger. The average life expectancy was six weeks. She prayed for the souls of scores of boys who would never return to County Leitrim and she prayed for their mothers who were condemned to outlive them. In Germany, Joachim's mother, Erika, mourned the men, too, but her loss was closer as early in the war, her brother was killed in France.

Joachim's father had marched into the war in 1914, riding his horse, Hans, and in those four years he fought on both fronts, lost many horses and many more men. He had witnessed what men became in war and he was bitter because he believed that the Armistice had been a trap. Germany would not, he believed, have lost the war had the politicians not abandoned them.

Paul, who had served as a captain, was disgusted by the German sailors in Kiel who mutinied, triggering a nationwide rebellion that pushed Kaiser Wilhelm II, the last German Emperor and King of Prussia, into exile and ultimately ended the war. An ardent monarchist, Paul believed that the rebels at Kiel embodied the threat of Communism.

Hitler capitalized on sentiments like the ones Paul had, fanning fears of Communism and the flames of discontent as he insisted that Germany did not lose the war militarily, but was "stabbed in the back" by politicians and communists. Although Paul judged Hitler to be a boor, he would later fight willingly for him as he came to believe that the brash Austrian would redeem Germany's reputation as a strong and sovereign nation.

The seeds of the next war were sown with the end of the last; there would be rampant inflation, staggering unemployment, a Great Depression, and from the ashes of defeat, Germany would rebuild and rearm. Joachim and Ted were destined to meet in the war that was, from the day they were born, inevitable. But first they would be boys, learning the values taught to them by their parents, their churches, and their schools.

Erika Müncheberg (née Ulrich) and Joachim.

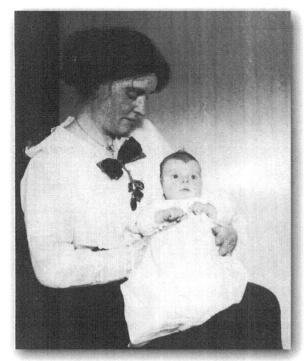

Nell Sweetland (née Reilly) and Ted.

CHAPTER 2

Born Lucky

———

THE HOMES TED AND JOACHIM lived in when they were children were built to accommodate different family sizes in very different geographical regions, but they also have some uncanny similarities. Though Ted's home was in an industrial city with a population of 32,000, and Joachim's was one of a small cluster of seven German farm families surrounded by acres of fields, both homes were two-story with multiple fireplaces and gabled windows, reflecting the prosperity of their owners. Paul Müncheberg and Ernest Sweetland worked hard to provide for their families, but they were also very lucky.

JOACHIM

For the Müncheberg family, 1919 had begun with the joyful birth of their son, but the following October the weather was miserable, Paul didn't have enough hands for the harvest and a sudden frost smothered the crop. Yesterday's furrows filled with fat-leafed potato plants were a sea of ice-crusted waves and Paul was in a foul mood when a neighbor arrived at his doorstep with Baron Jesko von Puttkamer who had brought along his young nephew.

The elder Von Puttkamer, a wealthy aristocrat, had already inquired about buying Paul's parents' property, which was not far down the road at Schönfeld, and they were in the region to view it. But it was noon, so first there was lunch and conversation, and by the end of the meal, the elder von Puttkamer decided he should buy Friedrichshof as well, for his nephew.

Joachim was ten months old, Eva-Brigitte two and a half, Paul had just lost half the crop, but lunch had lightened his mood. He wasn't really interested in selling the family estate, so he gave the Baron what he described in his memoir as a "joke of a price:" 800,000 Marks, the equivalent of well over a million US dollars today. To Paul's amazement, von Puttkamer was ready to make a deal.

Paul and Erika exchanged glances. With Paul's parents moving out of the area and his brother and sister already in Berlin, they had been talking about moving. Von Puttkamer's offer was too good to pass up so that afternoon Paul agreed: 400,000 RM now and the other half in two installments of 200,000 RM each.

The timing of the sale of Friedrichshof could not have been better for the Münchebergs. In 1919, the Reich Mark had not yet begun its inflationary death spiral and there were four Reich Marks to one US dollar. Within four years, Reich Marks were more valuable as wallpaper than currency; the archives are full of pictures of children using stacks of paper money like blocks, and the price of a cup of coffee could go from 5000 RM to 7000 before a customer had time to finish the first cup. By 1923, a single American dollar was worth over four *trillion* RM. Though he couldn't have anticipated what would come, Paul heeded the advice of bankers and moved his money into American dollars and real property.

With the final sale and the initial payment, the Müncheberg family and three members of the household staff began a series of happy moves, first to the Baltic coast where Paul bought a boarding house, then to a farm near Berlin, and finally to the bustling port city of Konigsberg in East Prussia. In the early twenties, as the democratically elected Weimar government attempted to implement policies that would boost the post-war economy, Paul bought East Prussia's only steel wool factory, a flourmill, a sawmill and a villa. While many Germans struggled to put bread on the table, the Müncheberg family joined the ranks of East Prussia's aristocracy. The age of the monarchy had ended with Germany's defeat in WWI, and Joachim's last name did not include "von" which would have signaled hereditary aristocratic lineage, but by association, young Joachim was one of the elite as he excelled in academics and athletics at the private school, which was attended by the children of the East Prussian nobility.

Later, Paul would write that those years in Konigsberg were the "happiest of our lives." Still when von Puttkamer declared bankruptcy, Paul Müncheberg was eager to buy Friedrichshof back for a fraction of what he had sold it for. In 1928, the family moved home again to the manor where Joachim was born on the last day of 1918. It would be the first—and last—home Joachim ever knew.

TED

Ted's home in Hazleton, Pennsylvania, was encircled by a wrought iron fence and a city block of manicured gardens and the house included enough bedrooms to easily accommodate the family, which had grown to seven children. The spacious mansion also included servants' quarters, and an inventor's workshop with a separate entrance. When it sold in 1928, the house was transformed into a maternity hospital, a quiet oasis in a bustling city.

Since his early days in Nevada's mining industry Ted's father, Ernest, had specialized in designing, patenting, and manufacturing industrial filters. He began with silver, but expanded to anything that needed filtration to reach its refined state: sugar and oil refineries, chemical plants and the food industries were available markets for Sweetland equipment. By 1926, Ernest was in a position to buy majority shares in United Filter Company, which had a workforce of over two hundred men in Hazleton; within a year, his patented filters were being manufactured and distributed worldwide, including in Halle, Germany.

Fortunately for Ernest, the relationship with his business partners, the Oliver family, frayed, so in 1928, he offered to buy them out. Oliver, believing that the price offered was under its real value, refused to sell. In a fortuitous move that echoes Paul's timely sale of Friedrichshof to Baron von Puttkamer, Ernest turned the tables and offered to sell his majority interest to Oliver at the same price he had been willing to pay. A deal was struck, Ernest cashed out and the family—all seven children ranging in age from 19 to 4, moved west to California.

The following year, on October 24, 1929, the stock market plunged, taking the value of United Filters stock with it. The Great Depression had begun, but while thousands of banks failed and millions of people lost their savings, their businesses and their homes, Ernest's sale of his shares in United Filters left him with only minor holdings in the stock market and the family's wealth remained largely intact.

As the economic catastrophe worsened worldwide, Ernest continued building as scheduled a grand French Norman style family home in the hills above San Francisco Bay. Features included leaded glass windows, forty-foot ceilings, hand-carved entry doors, a gold-leafed domed vestibule and an oak-paneled library with a marble fireplace; the surrounding gardens included a tennis court. It was the last move the family would make together and the last home Ted would ever know.

The manor house at Friedrichshof where Joachim was born and lived most of his life.

The Sweetland family home at 620 Church Street, in Hazleton, Pennsylvania.

The Müncheberg family home from about 1924-1928 in Konigsberg, East Prussia.

*In 1928, Ted moved to California where his father built
a family home in Piedmont, California.*

*Joachim and his sister with their nanny at Swinemünde,
on the Baltic Sea, circa 1919.*

Ted and his nanny on the Jersey Shore, circa 1921.

CHAPTER 3

Children at Play

———

TED AND JOACHIM WERE CHILDREN privileged to grow up in wealthy families with leisure time and opportunities. They both had dogs and played musical instruments, they both pretended to be cowboys and Indians, which was popular in Germany as well as America. They learned early how to ride horses and hunt; they played games of war and conquest.

JOACHIM

Children around the world play similar games, only the names and costumes of the rivals change, but for Joachim, who came from a long history of military service, there was an element of mimicry involved. His grandfather fought under Bismarck in the 1870-71 Franco-Prussian War and though he was seventy at the beginning of World War I, he regretted that he was considered too old to be sent into battle, but was assigned the "home task" of recruiting horses. Joachim's father was an officer in WWI and for nine years after the war, he donned the uniform of the monarchist leaning "Stahlhelm" charged with helping to patrol Germany's new border along the Polish Corridor. For Joachim the stories of valor, fellowship, and the glory of the military life were neither distant nor fictional.

Paul was proud of his war record and though we can't know the stories he told his young son, the memories he recorded years after the war provide us with his perspective, which is often as dispassionate as it is proud.

In the summer of 1914, the crown Prince Franz Ferdinand of Austria was murdered in Sarajevo. The news was unsettling for the whole world; one could sense the war had arrived. … I took my riding horse "Hans".… In the advance guard of the 4ᵗʰ infantry division we marched into Belgium via Aachen. The Wallonian citizens were vile; they attacked us from the rear as civilians – even a field hospital decorated with the Red Cross as a warning – every second man was shot. We were taking a mid-day rest in a neighboring village when we were shot at with a machine gun from out of a church tower. My soldiers climbed the tower and threw down a Catholic priest who had been shooting.

Sons are not destined to become their fathers, but they often echo what they observe. Long before Joachim was old enough to understand anything about the politics of Weimar Germany, he had absorbed something about what his parents felt. Paul and Erika were monarchists; they did not like, support, or trust the Weimar government, as they felt it had been imposed by the unfair Treaty of Versailles. Both Erika and Paul believed that Germany had not lost the war on military grounds. If they had been allowed to fight, they were certain they would have won, but the Armistice was signed in November 1918, and they were called home. Joachim could not have understood any of this, but nevertheless, when a representative of the new government came to visit, he made his stand. According to Paul's memoir:

The nanny entered with the children and greeted the men, Eva with a curtsy and Joachim with a bow and handshake. Only Joachim denied both to the county commission representative; he stood with his head erect and hands behind his back – he couldn't be moved to stretch out his hand. The man offered him chocolate, patted his head – nothing helped. Finally, he asked, "why don't you want to offer me your hand?" Joachim answered, "I won't give you my hand because you chased off the Emperor!"

The adults in the room froze. Paul wrote that it was as if lightning had struck. How would a representative of the new Weimar government react to a boy who had just revealed the family's solidarity with the monarchy that was no longer? Luckily the visitor found the young monarchist amusing, and though Joachim could not have understood what it meant to wish for the return of the Kaiser, nor would he have known the difference between an autocracy and democracy, he certainly demonstrated the ability to hold his ground. A kind of austere discipline also comes through in Paul's depiction of his son, who proudly wore his father's army uniform, which had been tailored to fit a small boy.

> *Our children were thriving. They attended Mrs. Lemke's private school and did well. Achim was a wild boy, war and Indian games took precedence, he was naturally the leader of his gang and there were many bumps and bruises. I erected an actual sentry box at the entrance to the yard where Achim stood for hours. Everyone who passed by had to give the password. The barracks were close-by so the soldiers marched by the house daily – Achim waited for the soldiers' return, placed himself in uniform at the head of the compartments and led them into the barracks to the soldiers' amusement.*

As his father wrote, Joachim was a natural leader among boys; he was also, it appears, extremely competitive. At school, he excelled, skipping at least two grades and even as a boy, he began to hone his natural athletic talents by diligently training. At Friedrichshof, his parents encouraged his dream to compete in the Olympics and made a track for him around the pond, complete with hurdles, a high jump and all ten events of the decathlon.

TED

When compared with Joachim's childhood, Ted's seems almost feral, though that's probably not fair. He was expected to do well in school, and he did well enough. With four older siblings, he was competitive, but also coddled as his older sisters took him under their wings.

At the same time, his early schooling was every bit as rote as it was for Joachim, as both the German and American pedagogy required memorization, without necessarily understanding. In America some progressive features were beginning to encourage students to discover problems on their own and hypothesize and test solutions, which is what Ted witnessed his father doing in the basement workshop. At school Ted learned, without questioning, a version of American history rooted in the experiences of the first European settlers (which included his great-great-great-great grandfather), the Founding Fathers, and the pioneers who headed west in covered wagons, his own grandmother among them. He was familiar with the general shape and geography of continents, and for Ted, the scope of North America was real as he had crossed it by train.

His father, a self-made millionaire, expected his children to work hard. When he was ten, Ted began to earn an allowance, which was tightly controlled and dependent on successful completion of designated chores. Ernest was strict; for him, there were no half-way measures and a job not done well was not worth paying for and Ted's income was not as regular as it might have been had he applied a little more diligence to his assigned tasks.

Like Joachim, Ted played cowboys and Indians, but cattle ranches with real cowboys were not far from Ted's experience in the American West, as the family had a second home at Lake Tahoe in the Sierra Nevada. It was there that Ted learned to shoot when he was not much taller than the rifle he steadied against his shoulder; he earned his first rifle when he was ten, and by the time he was a teenager, he was an excellent marksman and a practiced hunter.

Ted may have played soldier, since games of conquest are universal, but he certainly would not have stood for hours guarding a sentry box and no immediate family members were in the armed services. On the other hand, he knew the story about his great (times four) grandfather, John Sweetland, who enlisted in 1775 and was one of what Washington Irving called "John Glover's Amphibious Regiment of Marblehead fishermen" who helped get General George Washington across the Delaware, turning the tide of the American Revolution. Nobody knows if John was among the rowers, but he was definitely in the Marblehead Regiment and his story was proudly handed down from generation to generation, as was patriotism. His grandfather painted his lathe red, white and blue and though the colors gradually faded, it was unmistakably an American lathe which found its way to Ted's father's basement workshop.

Ted's wish lists for Santa perennially included war toys, graduating from popguns to tanks and field artillery cannons, which he creatively adapted to boost their trajectory. American Independence Day, the 4th of July, was a big picnic that featured impressive displays of fireworks, made even more spectacular with a specially designed fire cracker cannon that Ernest forged with the boys' help in the basement workshop.

The workshop itself was a place of business, but it was also a kind of inventive playground where Ted and his brothers were encouraged to use ingenuity, skill, and tools to design and build things. One project that consumed many hours was an attempt to create a candle that would burn colors like an open fire. Noting his interest in photography, Ernest built a dark room in the basement where Ted and his older brother spent hours experimenting with different chemical combinations to produce a variety of effects.

Freed from the necessity to contribute to the family income, and surrounded by love, Joachim and Ted had luxurious childhoods, full of exploration, play, and experimentation. When they were fourteen, they were still boys, still actively learning their place in the world, but in 1933, Adolf Hitler came to power, as did Franklin Delano Roosevelt and what they were learning had a lot to do with becoming citizens of the nations they served.

Joachim (center) and his friends playing American Indian games, which were popular in both Germany and the US.

Ted guarding his campsite in the Sierras.

Part Two:
Coming of Age 1933-1937

—

CHAPTER 4

Divided Societies

———

JOACHIM AND TED WERE WHITE, wealthy and Christian living in the United States and Germany; in both countries, even in graveyards, people were segregated by race and creed. As boys they could not help but sense that they belonged to a kind of elite. Unlike black Americans or German Jews, they were never excluded from restaurants, first-class carriages or any establishment they wanted to enter; there was no profession to which they could not aspire.

TED

Ernest John Sweetland was baptized in the Protestant Presbyterian tradition and in 1903, likely for business reasons, he became a Freemason, moving up the ranks to the 32nd degree.[5] Though the Freemasons are a fraternal organization and not a religion, Ernest's association with a traditionally anti-Catholic secret society would have been anathema to his Irish Catholic wife. Whatever the origin of his early allegiance to the Masons, his children were raised as Catholics. Like many Protestants, Ernest's family was deeply suspicious of his bride, Nell Reilly, her immigrant roots, and her allegiance to the Pope, who was considered a foreign despot. Still, her Catholic religion remained central to Nell's identity and she passed her faith on to her children, particularly Ted.

The household included people with different skin colors, but even as a very young child Ted would have observed that only the white people were invited to sit at the table. The black, Asian, and Latino people worked outside or in the kitchen or in the nursery, and the Supreme Court's "separate but equal" (1896) decision ensured that Ted's classmates did not include any black Americans. During Ted's lifetime American laws and traditions sorted people by race not only in schools, but also in trains, buses, many churches, on some sidewalks and in all branches of the US military.

JOACHIM

Joachim, too, lived in a patchwork society. The population of the Pomeranian province of West Prussia included a majority of Germans who were Protestant, ethnic Poles who were mostly Catholic, and a small number of Jews. The groups did not mingle. Joachim attended middle school in Falkenburg, where in the 1920s and early 30s, there was a synagogue, but it disappeared some-time after November 9, 1938, the "Night of the Broken Glass," a state-sanctioned pogrom against Jews. Spurred on by ordinary citizens, violence raged in the streets, Jews fled for their lives, and Jewish homes, schools, businesses and synagogues across Germany and the occupied territories were vandalized. Many of them, like the one in Falkenburg, closed and the congregation it had served disappeared. Years after the end of WWII, Joachim's nephew asked his mother if she noticed that Jews were missing. Eva's response to her son was simple: She had noticed, she said, because the shops were gone, but she did not ask any questions. No one did.

Asking questions is always dangerous and Hitler made certain to suppress all information that did not conform to Nazi ideology. Beginning immediately in 1933, the Propaganda Ministry, under the leadership of Joseph Goebbels, controlled all forms of communication: newspapers, magazines, broadcasting, and all publications. The crime of tuning into broadcasts from France or Great Britain was punishable by death as foreign broadcasts would undermine the Nazi version of the facts and Goebbels' philosophy was total immersion "The essence of propaganda consists in winning people over to an idea so sincerely, so vitally, that in the end they succumb to it utterly and can never escape from it."

In an autocracy, ideas that do not conform to the prevailing ideology are dangerous as is truth. Goebbels, who considered the press "a great keyboard on which the government can play" explained that effective propaganda speaks the language of the people with forceful persistence. In National Socialist Germany, the only stories anyone heard were chosen carefully and repeated endlessly by the government until the government's story became the people's perceived reality.

Hitler did not invent the idea of anti-Semitism, but he gave it a central place in the ideology and policy of the state. Joachim's sister was not the only Christian who opted not to engage in the risky behavior of asking questions. She was Lutheran and as Luther himself wrote, "Christ viewed the Jews as poisonous, bitter, vengeful, deceitful snakes, assassins, and the Devil's children....In his 1543 essay *On the Jews and Their Lies,* Luther branded the Jews a "plague of disgusting vermin."[6]

The Münchebergs regularly attended church services as Erika took Eva-Brigitte and Joachim to the nearby church in Wutzig, though in his memoir Paul wrote that he preferred hunting Sunday mornings. They were all good citizens, accustomed to obeying the laws, which increasingly made a person's legal status dependent on proof of their Aryan origins. As long as your lineage did not include any Jews, your rights remained unfettered.

For Christians, it was easy to go along with the state program as there was no organized opposition. Many churches were silent; some, as journalist William Shirer wrote, even heralded Nazism as a return to morality.[7] From their perspective, church leaders felt the Communists were a greater threat to religious freedom than Nazism, which is why they were not too alarmed when individuals who held communist, socialist, or democratic beliefs were deported or incarcerated in camps for political dissidents. As Erika suggested in her response to her son, it was better to go about daily business without asking too many questions.

Anyway, they lived in a bubble. Almost everyone they knew was "Aryan" and belonged to the Volksgemeinschaft, the "national community," and individual convictions—religious or personal—were subordinate to the laws and policies that bound the group. Their first allegiance was neither to God nor family, but to the Fatherland. Over time, even this would narrow as Hitler would demand allegiance to himself.

To be part of the community, one had to follow the rules, and there were many. Not long after the National Socialists consolidated power in 1933, telling jokes critical of the regime, listening to foreign broadcasts, allowing an elderly Jewish person to take your seat in the train—all were forbidden. Many offenses were punishable by death; all infractions would result in social isolation and the result was a "spiral of silence"[8] as ordinary Germans did not dare to air their questions, even to their own families.

The national community was exclusive and to be included it was necessary to prove Aryan racial purity, so documenting lineage became an important aspect of status and social promotion during the years of the Third Reich. It is not surprising that Joachim's father traced the family tree back to 1749, a project that proved an "Aryan" pedigree. In 1935, the Nuremberg Racial Laws were instituted and citizenship was revoked or denied for all Jews, who were defined not by religious association, but as someone with three or four Jewish grandparents regardless of their faith. Others described in racial biology terms as "blood foreigners" were also denied the status of Reich citizens.

In that same year, in a letter dated October 21, 1935, Paul Müncheberg's sister, Joachim's Aunt Louise, apparently responding to a request from her nephew to help with a school assignment about his family, wrote a twelve-page letter, a jumble of biblical quotes and righteous aphorisms, praising his grandparents as deeply Christian and saintly in their thoughts, words, and deeds.

> *... when I as daughter look back on the life of our father and think about some experiences, there was always only one thing that would "tip the balance" for him: the example of the life of Jesus. His whole personality was set in the service of his fellow men and highest fulfillment of duty in right deed and thought.... When your grandmother was a little girl, she learned the following from her father ... God is where the sun shines; God is where the violet blooms, where the birds sing, where the worm crawls; God is no person, God is not a friend to you, and does not lead you, your God is here ...The truth always speaks, and it never dares to lie. You can indeed deceive men, but never God. ... Hold on to God's Word: it is your joy on earth and as God lives, your joy will be in heaven. Scorn greatly the enemies who ridicule the church. When everything breaks and falls, the Word from God remains.*

It is not clear how Joachim reconciled that version of family history with the policies and practices of his National Socialist government.

TED

Nell Reilly Sweetland would have agreed with Aunt Louise: Her allegiance was first to her God. She prayed daily and attended Mass at least weekly and often more. Pope Pius XI had blessed her rosary and the medal with its knotted Celtic rim, which she wore around her neck: Mary, the Mother of God.

Prayer was part of her routine, and Ted sometimes joined her, though it's a stretch to think of Ted as remotely saintly; he was such an exuberant character, given to mischief and fond of practical jokes. Still, he and his mother were close. On occasion, he sat with her as she tuned into the popular radio show launched in 1926, hosted by the anti-Semitic Father Charles Coughlin. Though Coughlin's accent was Canadian, not Irish, and he was shunned by many of his fellow clergy, his mellifluous voice was soothing and his message appealed to many millions of American Catholics who knew only that he was a man of God. His Roman collar bestowed on him a moral authority that Nell's Irish Catholic education would not have questioned.

In the late twenties and early thirties, Father Coughlin was a fan of President Roosevelt and his social justice programs, but as time passed, his message shifted from supportive of FDR and the New Deal to isolationist, with vitriol aimed at all Jews and particular barbs thrown at Roosevelt and those he called his "Jewish conspirators." Sitting in the big wing-backed chair in front of the fireplace in the library Nell, who like Erika in Lutheran Germany, had long been conditioned to consider Jews agents of the devil and a threat to society, enjoyed Father Coughlin's weekly visits.[9] His message would not have been surprising. She was anti-Semitic for the same reason Father Coughlin was: Jews killed Jesus. That Jesus was a Jew was irrelevant to their argument.

In 1933, Pope Pius XI signed an agreement with Nazi Germany. If she read this Concordat at all, which she likely did not, or heard a distilled version on Sunday, she would have understood the agreement between her church and Hitler's government as simply codifying the natural order: the church was to engage itself in the spiritual realm, leaving all political and social agendas to the state. This was, in her world view, as it should be. That with its formal agreement the Catholic church gave legitimacy to the increasingly anti-Semitic, belligerent government of the Third Reich would not have occurred to her.

Decades later, the Church attempted to justify its position by parsing the difference between anti-Semitism and anti-Judaism. The church distanced itself from Anti-semitism, defined as hatred of Jews because of their race, but it allowed for anti-Judaism, which opposes Jews for religious and social reasons.[10] An anti-Judaic Catholic church could, therefore, admit converted Jews, but Hitler's anti-Semitic government excluded anyone with recent Jewish ancestry.

In any event, in the early thirties, the true extent of what would become the Holocaust was not evident to average Americans. Few Americans actually read Hitler's grand plan, *Mein Kampf* (1925) which provides hundreds of pages of rambling racism for the simple reason that Hitler would not allow it to be translated into English as "it would shock many in the West."[11]. The word "Endlösung," literally meaning "final solution" and used as a euphemism for genocide appeared in a Nazi Party plan in 1931, but neither Nell nor most Americans knew this.[12] The Concordat that Pope Pius XI signed with Hitler in 1933, did not, perhaps, make the Catholic Church complicit in the Holocaust, but it did eventually cause Catholics—and the world—to speculate about what might have happened had the church used the pulpit to inspire active resistance.

What Ted thought about his church's stand gets complicated when he gets older, but in the early thirties, he and his mother were very close, and the strength of their bond lay largely in the fact that of all her seven children, Ted was the most dedicated to the Catholic Church. Whatever the intent, the Concordat the Vatican signed with Germany in 1933 lent an air of respectability to the Nazi government of the Third Reich and in America, the broadcasts of Father Coughlin gave Catholics a way to legitimate anti-Semitism. As a young teenager at home in California, Ted would not have challenged either his mother or his church.

CHAPTER 5

The Year that Changed Everything

―――

TED AND JOACHIM

IN 1933, JOACHIM AND TED were in high school when their country's leaders changed and the boys' paths began to diverge more decidedly, looping deeply into the ideologies that informed the men they would become.

In Germany, Adolf Hitler began to dismantle the nascent parliamentary democracy of the Weimar Republic. In his first hundred days in office, he used a potent combination of fear, persuasion, and work projects to reduce unemployment, gain support for his programs and his party, and to build a vision of the great German "national community."

At the same time on the other side of the Atlantic, Franklin Delano Roosevelt was transforming America by implementing dozens of "New Deal" programs designed to mitigate the effects of the Great Depression. In his first hundred days, with the support of Congress, FDR won passage of twelve major laws that included ending Prohibition, building dams along the Tennessee River, and paying farmers to leave their fields fallow to boost prices of their crops.

In 1933, neither Ted's nor Joachim's parents supported their respective leaders. The Sweetlands were staunch Republicans, convinced that every American had an equal opportunity to benefit from hard work and were dismayed to find the newly elected Democrat increasing government involvement in the free market. Paul and Erika, thought Hitler was a boor, but they were not fans of the Weimar Republic's struggling parliamentary democracy either. As Paul wrote:

The situation in Germany was getting worse each year, economically and politically. The old Field Marshal Hindenburg was the President of the Reich; the bourgeoisie ruled more poorly than justly; the Communists and National Socialists publicly fought heatedly in brawls at political meetings and millions of people were unemployed in the streets when the National Socialists came to power under Hitler.

Initially, Joachim probably agreed with his parents, but as people were put to work and the economy improved, there was a burgeoning sense of national pride. In America, Ted probably agreed with his parents that the government should stay out of business, but at his high school, he was challenged to address the questions and problems that perennially plague humanity by taking a broader view. Later, after he graduated from high school, Ted wrote about his own education:

Under the Jesuit system of education, the student is taught some Classics … [after] he is given a background for his formation of ideas by the mandatory courses in philosophy. He is first taught the basic principles of logical thought, followed by a study of the great problems and their solutions. While Darwin, Kant, and Descartes, for example, were great thinkers, they differed from the conclusions arrived at by other equally great thinkers. Since truth is one, how is the bewildered student to know what is right if he has not been taught the principles of logic?[13]

At home Ted was taught the value of working hard, but he also knew that his parents continued to employ servants they no longer needed as his older siblings had moved out. Nell had grown up in the rooms above the pub in Carrigallen and the little house on Main Street in Carson City housed Ernest, his five siblings and his father's workshop. Ernest was a free market Republican, but he was not oblivious to the challenges of the working man in the Depression economy where jobs were scarce.

For Joachim and the generation of young Germans who came of age during the Third Reich, there would be no discussions about why great thinkers arrived at different conclusions or how these conclusions might be reasoned through or reconciled with one another. On the day that Adolf Hitler became Chancellor, there was only one worldview and it was framed by the narrow lens of National Socialism. Gradually, freedoms were being eroded, but in their place, there was security, at least for those who could prove their "Aryan" heritage, and a massive propaganda machine that relentlessly repeated what the State wanted its subjects to know and believe. Hitler was intent on building a single national community made strong by racial purity and a National Socialist world view. Joseph Goebbels, Minister of Enlightenment and Propaganda, was charged with promoting that world view through propaganda, a process that he detailed in a speech in 1928:

One cannot determine theoretically whether one propaganda is better than another. Rather, that propaganda is good that has the desired results, and that propaganda is bad that does not lead to the desired results. It does not matter how clever it is, for the task of propaganda is not to be clever, its task is to lead to success. I therefore avoid theoretical discussions about propaganda, for there is no point to it. Propaganda shows that it is good if over a certain period it can win over and fire up people for an idea. If it fails to do so, it is bad propaganda. If propaganda wins the people it wanted to win, it was presumably good, and if not, it was presumably bad. No one can say that your propaganda is too crude or low or brutal, or that it is not decent enough, for those are not the relevant criteria. Its purpose is not to be decent, or gentle, or weak, or modest; it is to be successful.[14]

Whatever else one can say about National Socialist propaganda, there is no doubt that over time, the messages put out by the Nazi Party were successful in connecting a disparate collection of individuals to National Socialist ideas.

To connect Hitler's ideas to a German intellectual history, Heinrich Hoffman, Hitler's personal photographer, staged a picture of the Führer looking at the bust of Fredrich Nietzsche, whose philosophy Hitler cited to justify war, aggression and domination for the sake of nationalistic self-glorification.[15] The Führer, however, was quite obviously not physically, intellectually or creatively the embodiment of Nietzsche's "ubermensch" (superior man) and Hitler denigrated any signs of "intellectualism" which he associated with Jews. Hitler was a master at manipulating masses with rhetorical flourishes, but the ramblings of *Mein Kampf* suggest that grasping complex intellectual concepts was not his forte and in any event, philosophical discussions did nothing to prepare the boy for the man he needed to become. As Hitler said, "Put young men in the army, whence they will return refreshed and cleaned of eight years of scholastic slime."[16] While textbooks would not be rewritten and reprinted until after Joachim had graduated in 1936, teachers were immediately reclassified as civil servants in 1933, and those who were not Aryan or not sufficiently enthusiastic about teaching the anti-intellectual ideology of the Nazi regime began to be removed from the classroom.

Both Joachim and Ted were "indoctrinated" inasmuch as the root of that word is the Latin verb "docēre" meaning to teach, but this statement is too simplistic. Every day parents and teachers are engaged in teaching their young how to behave in their world. Some of what is taught is overt, as books and experiences are selected for their content. Dialogue and body language influence how children think about what they're witnessing and this happens both consciously and sub-consciously. Indoctrination in the sense of the systematic transmission of values is a common and necessary practice, otherwise cultural continuity would be impossible, but there is a critical difference between a democratic system that allows inquiry and disagreement and a totalitarian system that does not.[17]

When he was fourteen, Ted attended Bellarmine College Preparatory, a Catholic boarding school for boys. The idea of education under the Jesuits was to learn to question, to discern, to doubt, to consider alternatives and finally to make a decision and act according to the principles of right reasoning. To be clear, Catholic education maintains that there are fixed truths, which are taught as doctrine. The Jesuits taught that truth is attainable and that man is a being with a spiritual soul, an intellect, and a free will. Ted was taught that man is destined for an eternal life and he operates towards that destiny through two powers: his intellect and his will. In the Catholic tradition, these truths are indisputable.

The role of a Jesuit education is, then, to furnish the intellect with the means to perceive, analyze and arrive at truth while developing habits that train the will to act in a way that leads to "good."[18] This form of indoctrination is designed to enhance the dignity and freedom of the individual within a framework of values that accepts the notion of man as a spiritual being who serves God.

The National Socialist world in which Joachim came of age also taught beliefs that they framed as "truth" but there is a critical difference. In the Nazi state, truth was manipulated to serve the state, so while Ted was learning that his role was to serve God, Joachim was learning to serve Hitler. Both boys were taught rules to live by, but the choices Joachim had were much more limited as he learned to serve as a vassal in a tyrannical state governed by regulations imposed on him and his entire generation "by promises of enticing reward, or by threats of severe punishment."[19] For Ted, reward or punishment would not be on this earth, but in the eternity that follows death.

In Hitler's Germany, the goal was to promote popular support of an agenda designed to lead to world domination. It was achieved by eliminating access to international and contrary points of view, spinning the facts through relentless use of propaganda, and enhancing the vision of a glorious future with pageantry that elevated Reich leaders to demigods. Those who furthered the goals of the Nazi state were publicly rewarded; those who dissented were ostracized, imprisoned or executed. The speed at which the National Socialist agenda was implemented, beginning when Joachim turned fourteen, is dizzying.

JOACHIM

Paul von Hindenburg, the aging president of the Weimar Republic, had been heavily lobbied by several interest groups to appoint Adolf Hitler as Chancellor of Germany. Conservatives of the former aristocratic ruling class thought that Hitler would fulfill his promise to destroy the republic, and in its place they believed they could appoint a conservative, maybe even a descendent of the Kaiser. Big bankers and industrialists like Krupp and I.G. Farben thought that Hitler would be good for business as he would keep Communism and the trade union movements in check. Even the military supported him as he promised to ignore the Treaty of Versailles and expand the armed services. Hindenburg and his vice-chancellor Franz von Papen believed that the angry little Austrian could not do any real harm as he presided over a cabinet with only three Nazis, including himself. As von Papen boasted to a colleague, "Within two months we will have pushed Hitler so far in the corner that he'll squeak."[20]

They had all underestimated the man and misread the people. A month after he was appointed Chancellor, a mysterious fire, likely ignited by Nazi activists, burned the Reichstag and Hitler used the charred wreckage to convince Germany's parliamentary body that the Communists were posing an immediate threat to the Reich. The only solution to this imminent danger, he declared, was to pass what was officially called a "Law for Removing the Distress of the People and Reich." This innocent sounding bill dubbed the "Enabling Act," essentially allowed Hitler to use the tools of democracy to dismantle democracy itself.

There was what appeared to be democracy in action, but it was fueled by terror. As the Reichstag was too severely damaged by the fire to provide a meeting place, members of parliament convened at the Kroll Opera House, which was surrounded by storm troopers chanting, "Full powers or else! We want the bill or fire and murder!" Only the Social Democrats refused to support the bill's passage, but all other members had been converted or were sufficiently cowed and the act that undermined their own power to check the Chancellor passed easily. Hitler became the omnipotent Führer and the Social Democratic Party, the only party that dared to oppose him, was outlawed. Democracy in Germany had collapsed.

As Chancellor and President, Adolf Hitler was holding all the cards, and though the Western press anticipated that Centrists in the Reichstag would limit his power, their optimism proved to be unfounded. The Reichstag, when consulted at all, was a rubber stamp organization. No party dared contradict the Führer lest they too be outlawed. Almost immediately after the Enabling Act was passed public demonstrations were illegal, free speech was banned and the right to privacy eliminated. This meant that officials had the right to read people's mail, listen in on telephone conversations, and search private homes without a warrant.[21]

In March of 1933, as Roosevelt celebrated his election victory in America, the first concentration camp for political prisoners was built in Germany;

April brought the secret police and the first boycott against Jewish-owned businesses. In May, thousands of "un-German" books were burned and "thousands upon thousands" gathered to hear Joseph Goebbels exhort students to clean up the "debris of the past." [22] Citizens everywhere were warned to eliminate work by "degenerate" authors, which included all Jewish writers and many Americans including Ernest Hemingway, whose portrait of German soldiers was insufficiently heroic, and Helen Keller whose apparent abilities contradicted the argument that it was legitimate to euthanize people because they had handicaps. By September, the press was nationalized and Jews were dismissed from all government jobs.

This series of events sounds catastrophic and eventually it was, but for Joachim and his classmates the day-to-day business of school at the Realgymnasium in Dramburg probably seemed unchanged. The rows of desks were as they always had been with the teacher scribbling worthy notes on the green chalkboard at the front of the room. Change would have been subtle: Jewish students were now required to attend separate schools and since Christian symbols were banned, there might have been a slight dusty shadow above the door where the crucifix had always hung. In its place, a picture of Hitler was to be prominently displayed; the swastika flag was to be raised, and the Hitler greeting was enforced.[23] Hitler, who had been baptized in the Catholic church, never denied Christ but he was not a practicing Catholic and he became adept at using Christian iconography for his own purposes—to position himself as Germany's figurative messiah.

None of this provoked controversy and western democracies stepped back. Germany was, after all, a sovereign nation, rooted in Christian morals and traditions. Nor did it seem to provoke any challenge from Joachim who, at fourteen, was a leader. In class pictures, he was often selected to carry the flag and on the field he was selected to compete on a national level. Young adults can be encouraged to ask a lot of questions as education everywhere is used to socialize and create identity, but in a dictatorship there is little room to challenge authority.

According to his father's account, as a little boy, Joachim had stood resolutely unwilling to extend his hand to a government official, but as a young man actively learning a new world order, such a stand in opposition to the state-appointed teacher at the front of the classroom would have been difficult, even unthinkable. Anyway, gifted both academically and athletically, Joachim had no cause to question the system in which he clearly thrived and he actively and apparently enthusiastically participated in state-sponsored activities.

TED

Ted was politically aware but unlike Joachim he was not politically engaged. In 1933, he was neither marching nor yet writing about what he observed politically though it's fair to assume that his views would not have been far from his parents, particularly his father who was a conservative Republican. Ernest supported Herbert Hoover's philosophy, which placed responsibility for achievement squarely on the individual who should neither request nor expect help from the government. It was clear, however, that the economy was not improving and three years after the initial stock market crash, with a win of 57 percent of the popular vote and 42 out of 48 states' electoral college votes, Franklin Delano Roosevelt's mandate was decisive. The Sweetland family, like families across the country, gathered around the large wooden radio shaped like a cathedral window and tuned in to FDR's inauguration speech broadcast live on March 4, 1933:[24]

> *This is preeminently the time to speak the truth, the whole truth, frankly and boldly. Nor need we shrink from honestly facing conditions in our country today. This great Nation will endure as it has endured, will revive and will prosper. So, first of all, let me assert my firm belief that the only thing we have to fear is fear itself—nameless, unreasoning, unjustified terror, which paralyzes needed efforts to convert retreat into advance.*

Thirty-six hours later, on Monday, on March 6, Roosevelt issued Presidential Proclamation 2039 closing the banks nationwide immediately. There would be no banking business for a week; no deposits, no withdrawals, no transactions of any kind. The order was issued in the middle of the night so Monday morning papers could carry the news. Radio broadcasters and newsboys shouting the headlines would be the first the public knew that the money they had deposited on Friday would not be available to them for a week.

What is striking about this unilateral midnight move by the federal government is that panic did not ensue; there were no riots or demonstrations. In the last three years of Hoover's administration, the Great Depression had taken hold; thousands of banks had failed leaving depositors with nothing to show for a lifetime of work; shantytowns dubbed "Hoovervilles" after the unpopular president appeared across the nation and nearly one of every four Americans was unemployed. Perhaps soothed by the confident voice of their new president in their homes, and frustrated by years of laissez-faire capitalism, businesses adapted and Americans waited.

The following Sunday, the Sweetland family gathered in the library once again to listen to Roosevelt's first "Fireside Chat." His voice was calm and his tone reassuring as he taught listeners a little about how banks worked and then informed them that while the banks were closed the previous week, their elected representatives, Republicans and Democrats alike, had come together to act on their behalf. Within three months, Congress passed the Banking Act of 1933, commonly known today by the names of the Senators who drafted it: Glass-Steagall. With the Depression in full swing, the act limited speculative investments by banks, provided for tighter regulation by the Federal Reserve, and most controversially, it provided deposit insurance through the newly formed Federal Deposit Insurance Corporation (FDIC).

Both the United States and Germany had leaders who were taking charge, but in Germany Hitler used the Reichstag fire to foment fear of the Communist threat and followed that up with a potent combination of intimidation and empty promises. If parliament gave him absolute power, he promised to end unemployment and pledged that there would be peace. In the United States executive power was checked by Congress, which had the power and the will to override the president, and they did. Despite FDR's opposition to the idea of a Federal Insurance Deposit Corporation (FDIC), Congress insisted on banking legislation that included insurance backed by the full faith and credit of the United States government. Over the president's opposition, Congress established the FDIC.

On both sides of the Atlantic the Great Depression had been devastating for ordinary people and they were ready to respond to strong leaders who were willing to act. In both the Democratic US and National Socialist Germany, those leaders wielded all the power they could muster. At school and at home

Joachim and Ted were learning how to make sense of it. The lessons were sometimes overt, but often they learned simply by observing how the adults around them acted and reacted.

JOACHIM

In 1933, Hitler's Sturmabteilung (SA) was a paramilitary branch of the National Socialist Party (NSDAP). The name means "Assault Division", and in the early days of the Nazi party, members of the SA were brown-shirted thugs who mostly intimidated voters, seized control of the streets, and squashed Hitler's political opponents. When their power exceeded their usefulness, Hitler authorized his personal bodyguards in the Schutzstaffel (SS) to collaborate with the Army and execute SA leadership. The purge of the SA leadership lasted several days, but June 30, 1934, became known as the "Night of the Long Knives" and was a powerful lesson to the German people. Over a hundred leaders who were seen as a threat to the Nazi regime were executed, mostly with guns, but the knife metaphor is clear: Hitler would excise any individual or group that threatened his leadership. As Hitler explained it to parliament the following month, "Everyone must know for all future time that if he raises his hand to strike the State, then certain death is his lot."[25] On July 3, the Reich Cabinet, all puppets of the Führer, issued a law legalizing the murders as a necessary emergency action to save nation.

Paul Müncheberg had never been one of the SA thugs, but he was a member of the "Stahlhelm", which was a nationalist paramilitary organization of WWI frontline soldiers and was until 1936, a part of the SA. After the family returned to Friedrichshof, he was on active duty patrolling the nearby border along the Polish Corridor. In Paul's recollection,

> *In 1933, the military district commander, a general, told us that twelve SA reserve troops were to be deployed in the Dramburg district; each of us was to establish a troop. I had reserve troop six. We were to recruit people from the war clubs where we were chairmen. We received military orders which had been those of the border patrol, that is, blowing up bridges, dismantling train tracks, maintaining the border until active*

troops arrived, etc. My troop had 200 men. The old Stahlhelm organiza-
tion still existed; our regional group had 83 men.

We don't know if Joachim accompanied his steel-helmeted father as he patrolled the border along the frontier that had once belonged to Germany, but we do know that Paul passed on to his son his nationalist views. The six-year-old who had worn his father's military uniform tailored to fit him grew up to be a teenager engaged in nationalist causes. During the summer of 1933, while Paul Müncheberg was establishing his troop of 200 men, Joachim traveled to Austria with the VDA, or *Verein für das Volkstum im Ausland* (Association for German Nationals Abroad), an organization that promoted German culture to ethnic Germans living abroad. Joachim would have been an able diplomat just by being himself—a bright-eyed young man who was also intelligent and athletic. Another photo in Joachim's album commemorates a summer demonstration in favor of the return of the Polish Corridor to the Fatherland. This would have been a cause that his father strongly supported.

A picture from Joachim's album memorializing his travels to Austria with the Association for German Nationals Abroad to promote German culture in 1933, five years before the Anschluss in which Austria was annexed by Germany. Small swastika flags fly above each banner.

In October 1933, long before the SA organization had been eviscerated on the Night of the Long Knives, Joachim also joined the SA for a very pragmatic reason: sports. The SA sponsored schools where competitive athletes could hone their skills. Going to these camps was selective, and a privilege, and even at fourteen, Joachim was an aspiring decathlete and competitive soccer player. The summer after he joined the group, Joachim traveled to two SA sports camps, one in Hammerstein and the other at the magnificent Rila Monastery in Bulgaria, which like many church properties during this era, had been appropriated by the state.

Joachim's photo album for these years is full of pictures of groups of boys playing together, often wearing similar outfits: a scarf, a shirt, or a badge that identifies them as a part of the larger group. They are pictures of belonging and conformity and a kind of wholeness created by the sum of the parts. During the Nazi years, the idea of "national community," (the "Volksgemeinschaft") was often described in biological terms as an organism with interdependent parts. The individual within that organism was not an autonomous being, but a part of the whole, which struggled daily against those who were its enemies, seeking to destroy it. Like young athletes in every country, through sports, Joachim trained and improved his own skills, while simultaneously learning the importance and value of being a part of a team. Physical education and competition was a foundational part of National Socialist pedagogy as it developed character, promoted self-discipline and the spirit of camaraderie through physical training. As Hitler wrote in *Mein Kampf*, character and performance should alone decide a person's value to the collective society. Even at fourteen, Joachim was by all measures, a valuable player, encouraged to compete and to lead.

TED

While Joachim joined groups of young people who were actively engaged in nationalist causes and learning that as athletes they had an important role to play in the emerging "national community" of the Third Reich, Ted was enjoying an American childhood that largely promoted individual achievement. To be sure, sports and competition were an integral part of Jesuit curriculum as "education of the whole person implies physical development in harmony with other aspects of the educational process."[26] Ted was a running back on the football team and was on the boxing team for which he trained diligently, but he suffered knee injuries that plagued him and, unlike Joachim, he did not distinguish himself in either sport. In college he took to the sidelines with his camera, and worked to find the best way to photograph players in action.

The family did not need additional income, but the Sweetland boys were encouraged from a very early age to use their hands to build things, ingenuity to make things work better, and business sense to figure out how to profit from an idea. Ted exhibited his entrepreneurial ambitions by launching a neighborhood dog-washing business, a suitably capitalist idea, though it was apparently heavily subsidized as the family's chauffeur drove Ted and his friend, Bill, to pick up and drop off their canine clients.

Like Joachim, at fourteen Ted was porous, absorbing every lesson taught by his parents, teachers, church, and environment. Like Joachim, he was academically and athletically able, but unlike Joachim he did not have a consuming interest in a particular sport and he was less disciplined, or perhaps less directed. Ted's father believed that being well read and "well rounded" mattered and Ted was free to dabble in whatever caught his interest and this suited his happy-go-lucky personality perfectly.

While Joachim spent much of his free time in organized activities, Ted enjoyed largely unstructured family time. Here Ted mimes "the big one that got away" after a fishing trip on Lake Tahoe.

CHAPTER 6

Belonging

———

JOACHIM

JOACHIM'S ROOTS WERE PRUSSIAN ON both his father and his mother's sides and his education, like Ted's, was largely rote, structured and ethnocentric. Unlike Ted's, however, education under the National Socialists focused on the creation of a single, pure, "Aryan" national identity and racial awareness as students were classified and sorted by race and ability. Joachim was clearly among the chosen. Throughout his secondary school years, he distinguished himself as a student, was a gifted athlete and a natural leader and he often appears in photos in positions of honor. Even as a young teenager, every activity prepared him to fulfill his duty to his national community.

Joachim knew that his father believed Germany had not lost WWI on the battlefield. As Goebbels' propaganda machine put it, the workers were inspired by the Communists to revolt and this action prompted politicians to stab Germany in the back by swindling the country into signing an armistice in November of 1918, forcing Kaiser Wilhelm II to abdicate his throne. The once powerful autocracy, embodied by the monarchy, was replaced with the messy uncertainty of participatory democracy.

For Paul and Erika Müncheberg the loss of a strong monarchy was wrong; for Joachim and his peers, the terrible retribution required by the Treaty of Versailles was an injustice that they would make right again. He and others like him were linked to one another in the single monolithic Volksgemeinschaft, the National Community. Otto von Bismarck's Second Reich died when the last Kaiser abdicated in 1918, seven weeks before Joachim was born. But fifteen years later, Joachim was taught that he and his whole generation would build the foundation for the Third Reich, which was clearly rising.

In 1935, Hitler unilaterally canceled the military clauses of the Treaty of Versailles and began remilitarizing the Rhineland. While preparing for war, street collections for winter relief to help the needy and public stew Sundays gave the impression of a state caring for all, a collection of ordinary people caring for one another. It was common knowledge, however, that the Volksgemeinschaft did not include everyone. They knew that the pennies they donated were not going to Jews or Roma or Sinti, nor would they would be going to help the handicapped. Their donations went only to people like them, whose physical and racial characteristics were acceptable.

But to be a part of the chosen! To fit, as Joachim surely did, among the sea of white faces, swastikas waving in ritualized celebrations that have distinctly Christian overtones and had an almost trance-like effect as they drew masses of people into the sense that they were an important part of the National Community, to which they owed their lives and their future. As William L. Shirer wrote, Hitler was the first politician to use film and gramophone records shouting from loudspeakers, reminding people of their misery, the impotence of the Republic, and the happy future that National Socialism would bring: more jobs for workers, higher prices for farmers, more business for businessmen, and a big army for the militarists. Shirer's description of the Nuremburg Rally is chilling:

> *200,000 party officials packed in the Zeppelin Wiese; 21,000 flags unfurled in the searchlights like a forest of weird trees. "We are strong and will get stronger" … Hitler shouted through the microphone… Jammed together like sardines, in one mass formation, the little men of Germany who have made Nazism possible achieved the highest state of being the Germanic man knows: the shedding of their individual souls and minds—with the personal responsibilities and doubts and problems—until under the mystic lights and at the sound of the magic words of the Austrian they were merged completely into the Germanic herd."[27]*

Leni Riefenstahl's film *Triumph of the Will*, authorized by Goebbels' pro-paganda ministry, immortalized the spectacular Nazi Rally of 1934, in Nuremburg where thousands of teenagers like Joachim were arranged like seraphim, clad in white, rapt, facing the miniscule figure of their Führer who spoke directly to them:

> *We want our people to remain strong.*
> *It will be hard and you must steel yourself in your youth.*
> *You must learn to suffer privation without crumbling once.*
> *And whatever we create today whatever we do*
> *We will die but Germany will live on in you.*
> *When there is nothing of us*
> *Then you must hold in your fists the flags that we hoisted out of nothing.*
> *And I know it cannot be otherwise*
> *Because you are the flesh of our flesh, blood of our blood*
> *And in your young heads burns the same spirit that rules us.*
> *You cannot be other than united with us*
> *And when the great columns of our movement march triumphantly*
> *Throughout Germany today I know you will join those columns.*

Joachim would be thrilled to hear Hitler's call. What young person would be immune to such praise? The National Socialist Party gave them purpose, direction, and an implied promise that their lives would be fulfilling.

Nazi education was designed to be a "total education" achieved by engaging youth at every age in a series of activities overseen by the state. This resulted in removing youth from the usual frames of reference by reducing their leisure time. Sports, which teach many positive skills, were part of this master plan as they provided a socially acceptable way to wean talented young people away from their churches and their families.

TED

Ted grew up dining at tables set with silver that had been extracted from Nevada's Comstock Lode. His high school was private and the curriculum was classical and rigorous, but the boys didn't wear uniforms and the formal school picture seems to indicate that the goal was discipline, not necessarily conformity.

Sports were a significant part of the educational program at Bellarmine College Preparatory, which Ted attended until he graduated in 1937. The school was proud to field a competitive football team, but while sports were part of his socialization, they didn't form quite the community that Joachim had. Mostly Ted spent time with two communities: his family, which he described as "the best in the world" and his church, which he attended faithfully, as expected. He was, like his mother, deeply religious, committed to the Catholic faith, but he was unlikely to be described as sanctimonious. He was the friendly one in the room who could not be ignored and he was a prankster, not above seeing what a cherry bomb would do to a mailbox. He was athletic; he swam, played tennis, and skied in the winter. He was a running back on his high school football team, but he was not a serious competitor and gave himself ample time to enjoy a rich social life in the city.

With his best friend, Bill Gallagher[28] who later became an artist himself, Ted frequented art galleries, critiqued movies, and had many conversations about their Catholic faith, which they shared, but also questioned. Perhaps inspired by Ernest Hemingway, who had also lived in the western US and whom he admired as a writer and outdoorsman, Ted joined the boxing team and a local gymnasium to improve his strength, but he wasn't as focused on boxing as he was on photography.

If history had been different, he might have taken photographs at the Olympic Games scheduled for Helsinki in 1940, where Joachim would have been running in the 100-meter dash, or hurling a shot put. Of course, by that time, Europe was at war and the games were not to be.

In the summer of 1934, Joachim (2ⁿᵈ from right, first row) attended the SA Sports School in Hammerstein.

Ted enjoyed photography and backpacking, which he often combined. This photo is taken near Benson Pass in the Sierra Nevada of California.

CHAPTER 7

The Olympics Showcase the Reich

———

IN 1936, JOACHIM GRADUATED FROM high school having completed all the requirements to attend university, a moment that was commemorated with many pictures in his album. Military service had become mandatory, but his participation in the SA (Sturmabteilung) and the Association for Germans Abroad (*Verein für das Volkstum im Ausland*) suggests that he would have joined anyway. At seventeen, Joachim enlisted in the army and volunteered to be considered for the prestigious, and selective, emerging Luftwaffe.

The year was a tumultuous one. In March 1936, in direct violation of the Treaty of Versailles, Germany remilitarized the Rhineland; in May, Germany's ally, Italy, invaded Ethiopia; and in July Civil War erupted in Spain, an eventuality that, to Goering's delight, would provide practice grounds for Germany's Air Force. The Luftwaffe's bombing of Guernica was in the future, but preparation for the Olympic Games had been masterfully completed and by August 1936, Berlin was a glittering showcase. Teams from around the globe were sent to participate in the grand spectacle of the XI Olympiad, their presence signaling a de facto endorsement of Hitler's Reich.

Joachim was among the participants, honored to have been chosen one of the 1500 athletes who represented the youth of Germany at the Olympic Games. Clad in white, heads held high, they marched into the stadium, showing a face of a new Germany—a Germany reborn, strong and youthful. Metaphorically connecting Germany with Classical Greece, the Berlin games were the first to begin with a torch, ignited in Olympia, Greece, then borne over twelve days by three thousand runners to the Opening Ceremony. For ten days of the Games, Joachim and hundreds of other young athletes camped in tents, competed with one another, and enjoyed the spectacle of some of the world's best athletes all striving for gold.

Forty-nine teams competed, more than in any previous Olympics; the two largest teams were Germany with 348 athletes and the United States with 312. Participation by the US was not inevitable as Jeremiah Mahoney, president of the Amateur Athletic Union, led an effort to boycott the games based on the radically racist, anti-Christian ideology of the Nazi regime, but the effort, supported only by a few politicians and the Catholic journal,[29] ultimately failed.

The American Olympic team included seven Jewish and eighteen African-American athletes who dominated the track and field events, which Joachim watched closely. From his photo album, it's clear that Joachim paid particular attention to the Decathlon, the event in which he aspired to compete in a future Olympics. He doubtless noted America's star athlete, Jesse Owens, and his remarkable performance as the young, black athlete sprinted and then took a long jump into history, defeating the popular German favorite, Luz Long. Long died in 1943, while fighting for Germany in World War II, but in a final letter to his friend Jesse Owens, he wrote, "Someday find my son ... tell him about how things can be between men on this Earth."[30]

At the Olympics, Germany presented the face of a nation that appeared to be thriving while the rest of the world was still struggling with the Great Depression. Unlike many other western countries including the US, most Germans were back at work building the Reich. Some of this was accomplished because of the manpower required to build Olympic venues, but there was more.There were certainly no visible clusters of men without jobs or families without homes; the city was clean and everyone seemed to have a job. There was, of course, no evidence of political dissent since people whose views disagreed with that of the government were labeled "antisocial" and they were sent to camps for "rehabilitation;" the media was controlled by the state, and no outside publications were allowed.

The Nuremberg Race Laws, though known, were not yet enforced so foreign visitors did not see yellow stars pinned to lapels, and all signs barring Jews from establishments were temporarily removed. Der Stürmer (The Striker), Julius Streicher's vitriolic anti-Semitic newspaper, allegedly the only paper Hitler read from cover to cover, was removed from newsstands as even the most casual reader would have been struck by the anti-Semitism it espoused. The world had come for a show and Joseph Goebbels and his propaganda team made the most of putting a solidly successful and benign face on National Socialism.

With the interlude of the Games over, and before he was required to report for duty in the army, Joachim spent two months in Luftmannshagen in the northern part of Pomerania not far from the Baltic Sea fulfilling his Reich Labor Service, which was compulsory and para-military. Training included a healthy dose of Nazi ideology and participants lived together in gray stone barracks-like buildings with rutted paths leading to the field where they performed military exercises before reporting for duty to help farmers and laborers clear land, or build roads.

Joachim's daily schedule during these years after high school was very different from Ted's. While Joachim had structure and clear direction into the military, Ted had moved into the exploratory academic environment of a liberal arts college. His father hoped he would pursue a practical degree in business or engineering like his two older brothers, but Ted was interested in neither of these pursuits and Ernest did not pressure him. He didn't attend any sports camps and compulsory military service was not yet instituted. For the most part, he was free to choose what he wanted to do and when he wanted to do it.

Joachim was honored to be among the youth selected to participate in the ceremonies at the Berlin Olympics in 1936. Based on the photos in his album, Joachim paid particular attention to the athletes participating in his chosen sport, the Decathlon.

In October and November, 1936, Joachim (second from left) did his part to "build the Reich" during his compulsory labor service in Luftmannshagen.

CHAPTER 8

Diverging Roads

———

IN 1937, WHILE TED WAS studying English at Santa Clara University just south of San Francisco, Joachim was studying the arts of war at the Air War School in Dresden. These two images stand in sharp contrast to one another. One young man was reading the Classics, pondering philosophy, taking photographs of football games for the school newspaper and writing short stories; the other was being trained, tested, forged in the discipline of the military. While Germany was preparing for war, America had side-stepped the role of world leader. The land of the free and home of the brave looked inward, unwilling, or as yet unable to accept the mantle of leadership that necessarily comes with power.

JOACHIM

In direct violation to the terms of the Treaty of Versailles, Hitler had been rebuilding the army, first in secret then openly for years. In Joachim's last year of gymnasium, German armed forces had supported Franco and the Nationalists in the Spanish Civil War. Just as Joachim was completing high school, Hitler instituted military conscription, but lessons had long been threaded with positive messages about war. Every student was required to read at least two or three war books and it was forbidden to have any critical discussion about the content of these books.

Even if military service hadn't been mandatory, Joachim likely would have followed the path trod by his father and his grandfather who were proud of their service, and whether or not they were required, he apparently read books about war, even for pleasure. As his nephew wrote:

I know that Achim read <u>Der Flieger von Tsingtao</u> by Gunther Plüschow, a Marine-pilot of World War I. Perhaps this man became an idol for Achim. I had this book from him in my youth as a gift from my grandfather [Paul] who also told me that his son had nearly all books—many of Karl May.

Karl May was a best-selling author in Germany and many of his novels were set in Ted's region of the world, the American West. The Old West stories feature a partnership between "Old Shatterhand," a German writer, and his "blood brother" Winnetou, an Apache chief, a kind of stereotypical Lone Ranger and Tonto relationship. May had never been to the United States and his fictional Winnetou is not so much an American Indian as he is an idealized German – noble, brave, and in the end Christian.

Whether or not Joachim saw Winnetou as a romanticized model or idolized Plüschow, the only WWI German pilot to escape from a British POW camp, it is clear that Joachim was an eager volunteer for the Luftwaffe. Watching planes take off and land at the airfield near Friedrichshof and flying when he was a young child with his cousin Hermann Hackbusch, a WWI pilot, had fired his imagination. When he was eighteen, he started to live the dream that had begun in childhood: he was learning to fly.

During his three months as an officer applicant at the Air War School in Dresden, Joachim met Heinz Hoffstätter, who became his best friend. Both young men were training as war pilots and as decathletes, hoping to be selected to compete for Germany in the Olympics. Joachim brought Heinz home to Friedrichshof where Paul prepared a training field for the "boys" as Joachim's mother, Erika, called them. We don't know if Joachim intended to play matchmaker when he introduced his sister, Eva-Brigitte, to Heinz, but the result was romance and in 1941, Joachim's best friend became his brother-in-law. The two looked remarkably alike. When trying to distinguish between them in a picture in Joachim's album, even Heinz's own sons (Joachim's nephews), had a hard time picking out which of the two blonds was their father.

Eventually, Joachim would become an Ace pilot, but his father tells an amusing story in his memoir about his son's early training, which was not going well.

I had a good time with the pilots on Sunday in Friedrichshof. I told the men of Achim, who had made a name for himself for his flight successes in the war, how his former commander had angrily attested during his training to be a pilot that Achim would never become a decent fighter pilot in his life; his landing in a practice flight had been so miserable, the commander would show him what a decent landing was and climbed into his machine and promptly made a crash landing. I had barely finished the story when all erupted into resounding laughter. The major who had been Achim's instructor and crash landed to show Joachim how to do it properly was sitting with us!

TED

From his dormitory at Santa Clara College, Ted had a view of the campus, which a student essayist described as "a semi-tropical park, with walks across which are cast the slender top-tufted shadows of regal, century-old palms..."[31] In the library, a short walk along graveled paths, Ted had access to several newspapers, which he read daily, a habit that had been encouraged in the Sweetland household where it was required that the front page be read before the comics or sports pages.

In April 1937, on the front page of the *Oakland Tribune*, news of the bombing of Guernica bled down the page: "Rebels Swoop on Guernica Mowing Down Women and Children Like Wheat." The "rebels" were not Spanish at all, they were, in fact, the Condor Legion of the German Luftwaffe. Under Hermann Goering's leadership, the Germans were using the Spanish Civil War to test a new aerial warfare technique: carpet-bombing. The little Basque village was a perfect site to determine how much power it would take to annihilate a town. The day and time had been carefully selected for maximum damage. It was Monday, market day, so many people were gathered in the village square. Under a hail of bombs and strafing lasting over three hours, the tiny Basque hamlet of Guernica was utterly destroyed. As Ted read, "The terrified civilians sought refuge in the hills, but the planes, flying low, turned machine guns on the shrieking populace, felling groups like a reaper going through wheat."[32] Over fifteen hundred people died and Goering would later call the experiment a success. In June, Pablo Picasso immortalized the awful moment in his massive painting using a palette nearly devoid of color but screaming with the rage of a mother holding her dead baby amidst a spectral rain of death.

During the following fall, as Nazi Germany and Fascist Italy supplied Spain's Nationalist rebels with firepower, Ted participated in a series of heated debates over whether or not the United States should remain neutral, a position that prohibited his country from exporting "arms, ammunition, and implements of war" to foreign nations at war. As the Spanish Civil War raged on, Japan was battering China, Germany was growing its arsenal and preparing for war, and undergraduates at Santa Clara argued whether or not "the earth was ready for another universal conflict." In November, Ted's debate team was assigned to defending neutrality, and they won, scoring high with the argument that "the huge expense of another war would sever the thread that holds the nations of the world from economic chaos." Their second argument was that dictators, like Hitler, would not take the risk of going to war.

Part Three:
Worlds Apart 1938 – 1940

———

CHAPTER 9

The Third Reich Expands

———

HITLER NEVER HID THE FACT that he was planning to build an empire where Jews were not welcome. In Mein Kampf he insists that Jews are

> *...a typical parasite, a sponger who like a noxious bacillus keeps spreading as soon as a favorable medium invites him...Wherever he appears, the host people dies out ...*" By the end of his rambling, he explains that WWI was lost because of the Jews. *"If at the beginning of the War and during the War twelve or fifteen thousand of these Hebrew corrupters of the people had been held under poison gas as happened to hundreds of thousands of our very best German workers in the field, the sacrifice of millions would not have been in vain.*[33]

The Nuremberg Laws, though instituted in 1935, were not strictly applied until after the show of the Olympic Games, but by 1938, enforcement was well underway. Jews could not own businesses, work for the government, or practice law; businesses owned by non-Jews dismissed their Jewish employees and Jews who were able to emigrate did so. Still, Germany needed more living space (lebensraum), so in addition to forcing Jews out, another part of Hitler's grand plan was border expansion. He would do this first by absorbing surrounding countries with significant German-speaking populations.

After months of sham diplomacy and Nazi activism, Germany's invasion of Austria began at dawn on March 12,1938, when German troops, tanks, and armored vehicles stormed across the border. The Nazi invasion was one day before a national plebiscite, which would have allowed Austrians themselves to vote on whether or not they should be an independent country, or annexed to Germany. By invading, Hitler prevented the vote from happening. In some Austrian cities, particularly where the Nazi Party activists including Joachim's youth group had prepared fertile ground, the troops were welcomed as heroes by Austria's seven million ethnic Germans.

The "liberation" of Austria was the only part of the story the German people were told and since it was forbidden to listen to international broadcasts or distribute media that held opposing points of view, the Nazi version of the "facts" was all they knew. The front page of German daily newspapers showed what looked like rioting in Vienna adjacent to a fake telegram from the Austrian Chancellor pleading for help from Germany to restore order.[34] International leaders must have known that Austria was being strong-armed with bully diplomacy liberally laced with threats of invasion, but the world response was just as it had been two years earlier when Hitler marched into the Rhineland: silence.

Joachim, who was already serving in the Army and hoping to be accepted into the elite Air Corps, was happy with the news of the "Anschluss" (annexation) as during his *Verein für das Volkstum im Ausland* (VDA) trip to Austria, he had observed the fervor with which ethnic Germans had welcomed their efforts to bring German culture to Austria. In school, he had been taught that all German-speaking peoples should be united under the Reich. Obviously, with so many people, Germany needed lebensraum (living space) and Hitler was fulfilling his promise to acquire it. At home, he had learned that the treaty that had ended his father's war was unfair so to ignore its terms was the right thing to do.

To Ted, and much of the rest of the world, it appeared that the Austrians themselves were delighted to have been invaded as thousands of Austrians took to the streets in spontaneous torchlight parades waving swastikas and Austrian soldiers linked arms with their German counterparts. But not everyone was celebrating. On March 13, 1938, the headline of Ted's local paper in California shouted, *"Germany, Austria United, Hitler Tells World; Nazi Soldiers Held 'Ready for Any Sacrifice.'"* The story led with Vienna hailing Nazi soldiers, but it went on to show another story unfolding in the shadows:

The jubilation in the Aryan section of the city, where all houses were brightly lighted, was in contrast to the Jewish quarter. Jewish shops were dark. Jewish homes looked deserted. Already excesses against the Jews were a forerunner of probable drastic measures to come.[35]

By 1938, nearly one of every four German Jews had emigrated, but the annexation of Austria brought another 185,000 under the Reich. Germany was pushing on the borders that had been imposed by the Treaty of Versailles, but the "drastic measures" against Jews did not yet include what the Nazis dubbed "The Final Solution." For its part, the United States imposed caps on immigration, leaving many Jewish families unable to flee across the Atlantic.

TED

While Joachim was serving in the Wehrmacht, progressing with a clear and ever-present goal to join the Luftwaffe in a world of structure and discipline, Ted was not at all sure what his career path would be. With the possibility that he might one day be able to make his living as a journalist, he chose English as a major, wrote for the school newspaper, and continued to develop his skills as a photographer.

Unlike Joachim, however, Ted's reality did not demand any commitments. He was not facing a requirement to serve in the military, and his family's financial circumstances gave him the luxury of an extended adolescence. Ted enjoyed an active social life and wasn't yet ready to take himself too seriously, but encouraged by his father, who lamented his own lack of formal education, he read widely. The oak paneled library in his Piedmont home included all the classics, several prizewinners and many bestsellers. In 1938, he read *I Found No Peace* by WWI war correspondent, Webb Miller, and Mark Twain's *Innocents Abroad,* a humorous assemblage of newspaper stories that chronicle an American traveling in Europe and the Holy Land.

Thinking that a career in journalism might be a good way to go, Ted kept diaries noting people and places and studied photographs to see what made them work. In the basement darkroom he made counterfeit press credentials for himself and his friend, Bill Gallagher, so that the two of them could go where they were not invited in San Francisco. Ted's father probably didn't know about the false identification, but it is clear Ernest thought that writing and photography were both fine hobbies, though he suggested that Ted might consider shifting his area of study to business, which he thought was a more practical path for earning a living.

His father's persuasion, however, was of the gentle kind and he was not insistent. Ernest enjoyed sitting in the library as the late afternoon light filtered through the leaded glass windows talking with his son about what he was reading or photography, an interest they shared. Often the conversation would veer into Ernest's adventures that included being run out of Mexico when the Revolution started in 1910. "It was dangerous," he said, "because they'd kill a man for his boots." Ted enjoyed those stories. He longed for a bit of adventure himself.

Two months after the Anschluss, Ted would have a different kind of adventure as he took a trip that would be unthinkable a year later: He spent the summer of 1938, in a Europe that would soon be devastated by the world's most devastating war. Ernest had financial interests on the continent as his filters were being manufactured in Belgium, France, and Germany but this trip was not for business. He told his four youngest children that he wanted to give them a "Grand Tour of Europe, while there was still a Europe to see."

On board Hamburg-America's steamer *The Roma*, Ted played in a table tennis tournament and "was thrashed soundly by a fellow named Rothschild." He worked out, took fencing lessons, competed in deck tennis and lost in the finals, won the shuffleboard contest and lost the bicycle race. Each night he dressed for dinner and "danced with every gal I could get my hands on." In his journal he noted with satisfaction that lemonade at the bar was ten cents and sandwiches were free.

On June 12, at 7:30 in the morning, Ted recorded their ship's passage through the Straits of Gibraltar.

To the South was Africa, seen thru an eerie haze. To the north, Spain. The rock is inside - at the side of a harbor. It is large, stone and dirt, populated and well reinforced—it doesn't seem as strong as it is supposed to be. We stopped there for about an hour. Peddlers rowed out to the boat and threw lines aboard on which to convey articles bought by the passengers.

A few hours later, Ted stood with a girl on the ship's deck as they passed Sardinia, rising in the moonlight like Plato's Atlantis. As they passed the Rock of Gibraltar, seas were calm, there was a cool breeze, and a full moon carved a glittering path across the calm sea.

The next time Ted chugged through the Straits of Gibraltar would be on a darkened ship as the Allies steamed towards North Africa, U-boats lurking in their wake. But on that warm summer night of 1938 as he sailed east to Mussolini's Italy, Ted couldn't know that future and he probably wasn't imagining it either. He wasn't thinking about the philosophy class he had just completed, or the shifting powers in Europe. Like any nineteen-year-old, he was thinking only about the moment and the girl by his side. Her name was Gloria and he described her as pretty and sweet.

The next day, they arrived in Naples. The family spent a month in Italy, touring in the Packard they had shipped from America. They dubbed their vehicle the "Queen Mary" because she was large enough to accommodate all six members of the family and their luggage, but hairpin turns on narrow roads built for horse carts and bicycles had to be taken in small bites by backing up several times. Throughout the family's summer abroad Ted kept a diary, and signaling the mark his Jesuit education left on him, the single line: *God is very good* ends every page like a feather of a prayer.

At Santa Clara, Ted's education was grounded in the Catholic faith and intellectual rigor. He knew himself to be a mortal being with a spiritual soul, an intellect, free will, and an eternal destiny. He was a member of the human community, which includes men and women of all races, cultures and religions. He was taught to see all human beings, whatever their creed or color, as children of God. But it is also likely that he was racist.

How could he not have been? Ted did not think of himself as sexist or racist, but he was both in the way that most white Americans were in the 1940's. His perspective was male and privileged; he had expressed surprise to see so many women "doing men's jobs" in Europe; he had gone to school with immigrant children, but never Americans with black skin. Even the armed forces were segregated by race. As the historian Stephen Ambrose wrote about American democracy pitted against Hitler's Nazis, "The world's greatest democracy fought the world's greatest racist with a segregated army."[36]

Americans have always separated themselves into groups—sometimes by choice, often not. We separate ourselves by our apparent physical characteristics: race, gender, age. But we also sort ourselves into various hierarchies by education, religion, ethnicity, and wealth. As a first generation Irish Catholic immigrant, Ted's mother knew that Ernest's Nevada Protestant family did not consider her his equal. Those instincts to separate ourselves from people who look or think differently have not gone away and though decades have passed, the seeds of prejudice continue to be fanned by leaders who wield our common language like an ax to divide us.

At Santa Clara, all of the students were boys and most were white and Catholic, but there were Protestants and Jews in attendance, segregated only in that they were not required to take the religion class that focused solely on Catholic theology. In their academic courses Ted and his fellow students were challenged to develop their intellects to find truth, and exercise their will to do good. This ambition is as grand as it is vague. What does it mean to "do good"? Was Joachim "doing good" by doing his duty to his Führer because it was required? Is obedience in itself always good?

It's the kind of question Ted and his classmates would have discussed, perhaps with one of Santa Clara's most popular teachers, Father Austin Fagothey, who later synthesized his classes in the book *Right and Reason,* which explores many of these ideas. There are no easy answers to such questions, but Ted's education would have provided him with certain premises: good and evil, moral responsibility, moral obligation and heroic acts all exist in this world. Living a "good life" means exercising free will to live in a way that intentionally navigates those truths. In 1940, Santa Clara's President wrote that a Jesuit education is grounded in faith and it "Rejects Racism, Communism, Nazism, Fascism, or any other system of Philosophy or of government which denies to men his human dignity and human rights."[37]

In his journal, in which he wrote every day during his summer travels, Ted writes about Italian peasants walking with staggering loads and "the number of very small children doing a man's work." Ted's journal rambles stolidly through Italy from Naples across the Amalfi Coast to Salerno, where twenty years earlier Allied soldiers in WWI had "shot propaganda shells with leaflets telling the Germans to surrender and fired high explosive shells to help them make up their mind."[38]

In Ravello, Ted notes that its beauty inspired Wagner to write *Parsifal*; in Rome, he wrote that Mussolini's villa was "magnificent, beautiful, marvelous" and upon observing the Fascist Youth Center, he remarked that the Italian Dictator "is very intelligent. He rewards good physical accomplishments and in that way breeds a strong and very satisfied nation. All the Italians seem to like him extremely...." Ted did not pass judgment on the man himself, and anyway as a nineteen-year-old Catholic, he may have thought that Benito Mussolini was a good man. Italy was officially Catholic and its Fascist dictator was theoretically a friend of the church.

The highlight of Ted's Italian trip was June 25. On that day he would, along with scores of other faithful, enjoy a relatively private audience with Pope Pius XI at his summer residence in the hills not far from Rome. Ted lingered on the beautiful grounds of the Castel Gandolfo and marveled at the beauty of the villa perched above Lake Alban. In his pocket, he cradled the medal his parents had given him for his nineteenth birthday. It was not a talisman, but the round gold medal with an embossed image of Christ would be blessed by the Pope and Ted would treasure it for the rest of his life.

As he waited for His Holiness to emerge, Ted could not have known that on that very day, Pope Pius XI had met with the American Jesuit priest who was also a journalist, John LaFarge. The Pope had read LaFarge's book, *Interracial Justice: A Study of the Catholic Doctrine of Race Relations*, and the Pope wanted the Jesuit journalist to work on a document that could provide background for an encyclical on the unity of the human race. His intention was to go beyond his 1937 letter, *Mit Brennender Sorge,* (With Burning Concern) in which he denounced the most virulent forms of racism, but stopped short of condemning Nazi policies generally.

Unfortunately for him and for Jews worldwide the night before Pius XI was scheduled to call Catholics to speak and write and act against what was happening in the Third Reich, he died. The timing of his death is interesting and had Ted lived, he might have penned a mystery set in the Vatican in early 1939. But whatever imagination might add to the sketchy circumstances of the pope's death, one thing is true: The work Pope Pius XI had begun with John LaFarge in the summer of 1938 was buried in the archives, and on the issue of human rights in Germany, his successor, Pius XII, is remembered mostly for his silence.

In Florence, Ted met Charles Evans Hughes, the Chief Justice of the Supreme Court, who had been his father's attorney in 1931, in a patent infringement lawsuit Sweetland had filed against the auto giant, General Motors. By the time this "David and Goliath" case was appealed all the way to the Supreme Court, Hughes was Chief Justice and recused himself, but the court stood by the original decision: The lone, independent inventor had beaten GM. While Chief Justice Hughes had played a part in family history, Ted was more excited when he saw the King of Spain, Alfonso XIII, at Lake Como. He didn't take any pictures of the king by the lake, but if he had, the caption might have noted that while the king was enjoying a peaceful exile at Lake Como, the Spanish Civil War was raging.

After spending a month in Italy, the family drove across the border into Switzerland where they enjoyed a mid-day picnic near a waterfall, climbed St. Gotthard's pass and ended the day at the Hotel Meyerhof. Ted wrote that his younger siblings, Helen (15) and Gene (14), *spent two weeks in the room where Queen Victoria slept in 1880. What fun—are they proud!"*

In his diary, in which he faithfully recorded his location, meals, and sights, Ted did not engage in speculation about politics, but he no doubt knew about the international conference that was going on as he and his family lumbered in the Packard across Switzerland to Paris. At Evian, not far off the Sweetland's touring route, thirty-two international delegates were meeting to discuss the Jewish refugee crisis. Nazi policies were designed to hasten their departure, and by July 1938, one in every four German Jews had already fled from Germany. The annexation of Austria brought more Jews under Nazi rule, but after nine days of meetings, countries remained closed. Except for the tiny nations of the Dominican Republic and Costa Rica, no country was willing to accept desperate refugees who would soon be fleeing for their lives. Nor did any church, Catholic or Protestant, step up. The Jews were isolated, trapped in the Third Reich, and were not considered to be any other country's problem.

The world did not yet seem to understand the full extent of the Nazi agenda. They were being marginalized, demonized, and encouraged to emigrate, but they were not yet being executed en masse, and in much of the world, including the United States, anti-Semitism was not uncommon.

Ted's photos of the trip include a few pictures of family, but mostly the pictures are like postcards, snapshots of beautiful or iconic places: The Eiffel Tower in Paris, St. Mark's Square in Venice, the Changing of the Guard at St. James Square in London. The diary and pictures tell a story, but of places, not of people, and his notes are journalistic and cryptic as if he was planning to write more later:

None of the European hotels provide soap, you must furnish your own...
All of the countries are preparing for war as best they can, no trouble or
cannon fodder spared...War is hell.

After three months of travel through Italy, France, Switzerland, England and Scotland, Ted and family boarded the *S.S. Hausa,* and returned to the US. In September, shortly after Ted's classes resumed at Santa Clara, statesmen from Great Britain, France, and Italy met with Hitler in Munich. There, in exchange for a promise of what the British Prime Minister, Neville Chamberlain, called "peace in our time" they sliced the Sudetenland off the sovereign nation of Czechoslovakia and gave it to Germany. Czechoslovakia had a choice: they could either submit to the agreement or they could go to war alone against Germany.

JOACHIM

To Hitler's delight, Czechoslovakia chose to submit to the Munich agreement, which had been drafted by Prime Minister Benito Mussolini of Italy who, though not yet a formal ally with Germany, was not at arms distance either. Two years later, when it seemed clear that Hitler would triumph, Mussolini would join him in the Axis alliance with Japan.

The Munich agreement Mussolini crafted gave Nazi Germany everything Hitler wanted and was celebrated there as a feat of diplomacy, as it was in

Britain, where it was quite wrongly assumed that war had been averted. On the night of September 30, 1938, Chamberlain returned from Munich to England and announced to the crowd gathered at #10 Downing Street:

> *My good friends, for the second time in our history, a British Prime Minister has returned from Germany bringing peace with honor. I believe it is peace for our time...Go home and get a nice quiet sleep.*

He was wrong. Hitler had simply knocked a knight off the chessboard. Czechoslovakia had been militarily strong; its Air Force posed a threat to Germany's own resources; and the Sudetenland itself contained sixty-six percent of Czechoslovakia's coal, seventy percent of its iron and steel, and seventy percent of its electrical power. With a stroke of a pen, Britain and France emasculated a potential ally with a well-trained military. Later, many Czech pilots who were able to escape their own country joined the Royal Air Force to fight the Nazis.

At the time of the Munich Agreement, Joachim was in the Wehrmacht, but his application to join the Luftwaffe had not yet been accepted. He was a decathlete, and according to Nazi race theory he was "physically and eugenically" sound, but acceptance to the elite Air Force was by no means certain. In a book originally published in 1943, purportedly by a Nazi insider under a pseudonym that remains mysterious, "Hauptman Hermann" describes the process:

> *The Nazis took great care to earmark the best human material for the Luftwaffe. Only volunteers were considered. There was never any attempt at drafting for the Luftwaffe. Even of the volunteers only about 50-60% proved qualified physically and psychologically. Of these again about half had to be retired after the first flights. Of those who were finally sent to pilot schools, a great many never even got so far as to solo, let alone to reach their final flight tests. And the tests, in turn, revealed that some of those who had come that far had good technical knowledge but weren't good pilots.*

Joachim was one who was found to be sound in body and mind. In October 1938, he was officially admitted to the Luftwaffe and shortly after, he began training at the Fighter Pilot School in Werneuchen. Training for the Luftwaffe was compressed by design because, though they needed pilots, the Nazis wanted to "let young people loose before they have calmed down, which they invariably do during a long training period."[39] Apparently Joachim had what it took to be a successful pilot because in less than a month, he not only had his wings, but was promoted to Second Lieutenant.

The day after Joachim's promotion, November 9, 1938, would become known as "Kristallnacht," which literally means "Night of Crystal" and is often referred to as the "Night of the Broken Glass." For two days and nights throughout Germany, Austria, and Czechoslovakia's Sudetenland, Jewish shops were vandalized, 267 synagogues were burned and tens of thousands of Jews, mostly men, were taken to concentration camps. It is not possible that Joachim was unaware of these events, which were officially sanctioned by the government he had volunteered to serve, but it is also not possible to know how he thought or felt about them. It is clear, however, that he did not deviate from his chosen path; he would continue to follow the leader he had sworn to serve.

The summer of 1938, Joachim (back row, second from left) attended fighter pilot school in Dresden.

The summer of 1938, Ted toured Europe with his family in a Packard.

Ted in Italy in 1938, with his younger brother, Gene, my father.

"Big help in the garden" – Joachim and Heinz Hoffstätter, his future brother-in-law at Friedrichshof, taking a break from War School.

CHAPTER 10

The Time Has Come ...

———

The Walrus and the Carpenter
Walked on a mile or so,
And then they rested on a rock
Conveniently low:
And all the little Oysters stood
And waited in a row.

"The time has come," the Walrus said,
"To talk of many things:
Of shoes--and ships--and sealing-wax--
Of cabbages--and kings--
And why the sea is boiling hot--
And whether pigs have wings."

LEWIS CARROLL, 1872
EXCERPT FROM *THE WALRUS AND THE CARPENTER*

TED

IN JANUARY 1939, SIX MONTHS after he returned from his travels in Europe, Ted began writing for the weekly campus newspaper, *Santa Clara*. He dubbed his column "Cabbages and Kings," a phrase he borrowed from Lewis Carroll's poem that has an amusing tone, an upbeat rhyme and makes light of a generation of oysters plucked for the slaughter. Ted enjoyed a good joke and clever poetry, and he used humor to mask the gravity of issues that he knew to be deadly serious. Perhaps in naming his column, he was thinking of himself and his generation as the drumbeats of war began to sound. In his first column he skimmed lightly across the Spanish Civil War, where Franco's Nazi-supported Nationalists were fighting the Communist-supported Republicans; he touched on tensions between Italy and France, China and Japan, and ended with a mild rebuke for Britain, the great appeaser.

> *It looks like the two naughty children in the Spanish corner of the nursery are at last going to stop breaking each other's toys. At the cost of 1,000,000 lives, a year and a half of progress, and countless years of civilization, Franco has one more doll to break—a beautiful (and rugged!) one, Barcelona.*
>
> *...Now if Muss will stop jumping on France's toes and Hitler will just suck his thumb a while longer, everything will at last be quiet—that is, if Japan and China kiss and make up and the overstuffed British calico lion stops licking the children's hands!*

Ted was a reader of books, newspapers, and magazines. He was well aware of what was happening in Europe, but there was a great chasm between his life on Santa Clara's idyllic campus and what the newspapers informed him was occurring elsewhere. Sometimes his columns seem callow as he seemed to make light of things that became deadly serious. Then again, perhaps a little like Lewis Carroll, Ted used humor to pull back, to gain perspective, and ultimately to make sense of a world that seemed to be shattering. In his later writing, even when death was close, humor was a frequently used weapon in his mental arsenal.

Ted must have known that Jews were being marginalized, persecuted, and denied the ability to make a living, but what he thought about it remains a mystery. Even Kristallnacht didn't provoke moral outrage by the Catholic Church or democracies worldwide and Ted did not write about any of it. The only hint we have that he and his fellow students might have recognized the difficult position of the Catholic Pope in a Fascist country aligned with Nazi Germany is the eulogy published in the college newspaper in 1939, when Pope Pius XI died. *"Last week there passed away simply and peacefully a troubled old man whose heart was so full of the miseries and afflictions of this world that his last words were these sad and regretful ones: "And there is so much to do!"*[40]

There was much to do, but neither state nor church leaders were doing much. Following Kristallnacht in November 1938, the United States had brought Ambassador Hugh Wilson home, but that was it. No other country reacted; diplomatic relations continued and borders remained closed to nearly 400,000 Jews within the sphere of the Third Reich whose assets were being confiscated while they were being charged an "atonement fine" to pay for the damage the Nazis had caused. By the beginning of 1939, Jews could no longer drive cars, use public transportation, or go to public parks, museums, plays or concerts. All of this, the world knew. but in his speech to the Reichstag on January 30, 1939, Hitler blames the Jews.

> *"Once again the international Jews are plunging the world into war. They will bring about the destruction of the Jews in the end. The creators of the land have to recognize her common enemy. Germany wants to be free!"*[41]

The Reichstag erupted in applause. The rest of the world remained huddled in silence. There was, after all, no war. Not yet. Two months after Hitler's Reichstag speech and six months after the "peace for our time" Munich agreement, German forces marched into Czechoslovakia and took the rest of the country, including Moravia and Bohemia. As Germany had disbanded Czechoslovakia's military when they took over the Sudetenland, the occupation was bloodless. Five days later, Lithuania was forced to give up the former Prussian Memel Territory. Only tiny, unsupported Romania held on to the thread of neutrality. Poland was doomed.

Two weeks after Germany had redrawn the map of Eastern Europe, Ted wrote in his column with his typical sardonic tone intact:

> *I like Hitler. I think he's a swell fellow. … While the democracies are fluttering around with umbrellas and cabinets, the little fellow with a blob of mustache grabs what he wants, and does his talking afterward.*
>
> *Chivalry is still alive, the strong still take it from the weak, and the wise still take it from the strong. One who is both wise and strong has a*

great advantage over the others; whether there is such a rare person in Europe remains to be seen.

Ted goes on to synthesize an editorial from one of the local San Francisco Bay Area metropolitan daily papers: *Hitler is a maniac...We need to be prepared to fight...Democracy is being imperiled.* But he reads these observations as a skeptic suggesting an isolationist leaning and he ends with this: *Marvelous how the public is being fattened just in case they will be needed for the sacrifice on Mars' altar.*

The slicing up of Europe was not yet Ted's war. He was not yet morally outraged. His was the generation that would be served up like the little marching oysters for the slaughter, but it was not a fate that he thought was inevitable. At the same time, he was not oblivious to the risks, as he took in the sweeping vista of San Francisco Bay from the top of Nob Hill.

A young lady and myself had just agreed that the new rearmament program was a ridiculous waste of money, as we were about to enter a large San Francisco hotel for an evening of dancing. The searchlights of the battleships in the harbor were prying about the heavens, when suddenly a huge bomber was outlined in the gloom. Suppose it was an enemy bomber!

JOACHIM

In 1939, while Ted was musing in print, a massive propaganda campaign was sweeping across Germany, ensuring the allegiance of youth, but Joachim was already nineteen and learning the art of the fighter pilot. When Czechoslovakia was trampled without having to deploy the Luftwaffe, he may have been disappointed. He was ready for action and eager to prove himself in the war they all knew was coming. Joachim's commander, Hermann Göring, was certainly disappointed by the bloodless occupation. As he wrote:

"The political genius of our Führer unfortunately has seen to it that we will not have the satisfaction of a great war now. But I still hope that one day I will be able to march into Berlin at the head of a victorious Luftwaffe."[42]

Hitler had cowed the small countries into submission but there was one more chess piece to neutralize before he could start the Great War for which Göring had hoped. The colossal Soviet Union had to be defanged, but Hitler and Stalin certainly did not make for natural allies. A key theme of Nazi education was anti-Bolshevism, which was a blight on the National Community and, left unchecked, would creep like a cancer across Russia's borders and destroy Europe. Communists in Kiel were conveniently blamed for the loss of WWI and concentration camps were full of prisoners whose only crime was to be Communist.

Stalin loathed Fascism as much as Hitler hated Communism, but Stalin was not happy that Britain, France and Italy had left him out of the negotiations as they wrote and signed the Munich agreement, so he placed the massive might of the Soviet Union exactly where Hitler needed him—effectively neutralized. In exchange, the Soviet Union would sweep the Balkans within their sphere of influence. On August 24, 1939, the two dictators signed a mutually beneficial Nonaggression Pact in which they agreed to take no military action against each other for the next ten years. Neither of these despots were in the habit of making promises they intended to keep, and not consulting the Italians about the new partnership would prove to be a costly mistake for Hitler, but the immediate effect of the pact assured Hitler that the Wehrmacht could invade Poland without being threatened from the East. In fact, the Soviets would assist in guiding the Luftwaffe to their targets in Poland by keeping their radio signal going from Minsk; a signal that navigators could pick up easily to get their bearings.

The stage was set for a "blitzkrieg" of Poland—a lightening war of shock and awe that would terrorize the population, destroy targets and end quickly. In fact, they were so confident that their strategy would work, the Nazis did not implement a logistical plan to repair or replace damaged equipment because they believed the war would be over before repaired equipment would be needed—and they were right. At least, at the beginning.

On September 1, 1939, under the guise of quelling unrest that they had instigated themselves, Germany marched into Poland. This time, the Allies did not stand down. This was a surprise as Hitler was in the habit of seeing France and Britain acquiesce. In 1935, they had accepted Germany's rearmament, in

1936 they accepted occupation of the Rhineland and in March of 1938 they didn't flinch when Austria was annexed and the following September, a piece of Czechoslovakia was amputated followed by the occupation of the whole country. Wilhelm Keitel, the Supreme Commander of Germany's Armed Forces, put it this way, "Britain was too decadent, France too degenerate, and America too uninterested to fight for Poland." [43]

Many of their conclusions were correct. The public in the West had been treated to a spectacular show at the 1936 Olympics—Germany had emerged from economic catastrophe and had become a beacon of success. The West was not eager for a reprise of 1914-1918; many felt that the terms of the Treaty of Versailles were too punitive in the first place and the general consensus was that communism was a much greater threat than fascism. On the other hand, with the bloody invasion of Poland, Britain finally realized that the devil could not be appeased. On September 3, 1939, Prime Minister Neville Chamberlain addressed the whole of the United Kingdom from the Cabinet Room at Number 10, Downing Street:

We and France are today, in fulfillment of our obligations, going to the aid of Poland, who is so bravely resisting this wicked and unprovoked attack upon her people. We have a clear conscience. We have done all that any country could do to establish peace, but a situation in which no word given by Germany's ruler could be trusted and no people or country could feel themselves safe had become intolerable. And now that we have resolved to finish it, I know that you will all play your part with calmness and courage.

At such a moment as this the assurances of support that we have received from the Empire are a source of profound encouragement to us.

...Now may God bless you all and may He defend the right. For it is evil things that we shall be fighting against, brute force, bad faith, injustice, oppression and persecution. And against them I am certain that the right will prevail.

In Germany, this day, September 3, not their army's September 1 invasion of Poland, would be noted as the first day of a war that was started, they insisted, by Britain. Joachim and all Germans would only know the part of the story that the Nazi government wanted them to know and propaganda under Joseph Goebbels' able leadership would embellish the tale: The Nazis were simply counter-attacking. The Führer had, Goebbels wrote, made many overtures inviting peace, but in the face of the British threat, Germany had to retaliate. It was their duty to defend the Fatherland.

TED

Ted was at his desk in his dorm room when Edward R. Murrow broadcast the news that early Sunday morning, September 3, 1939, Britain had declared war on Germany. Ted leaned into his radio to listen. He lit the pipe he had bought for himself in Switzerland and began to write his weekly column.

> *It was 11:13 o'clock Sunday, September 3. A tall, gaunt man was sitting in the cabinet room, Number 10 Downing Street. He was alone. The only light in the room was a single desk lamp that left the shadow of the empty cabinet chairs pale specters outside the cone of light. Beyond the building the regular nocturnal street noises murmured.*
>
> *In other rooms of the building a muffled commotion was going on; last minute preparations were being made, papers were being signed, matters being concluded. This man seemed completely isolated, like a matchstick in a quiet pool beside a swirling stream. In front of him was a microphone, the focal point of a clutter of papers, reports, books, and dispatches.*
>
> *The nervous fingers of this man played over the sensitive surface of the mechanical ear, prepared in two minutes to tell millions of people in thousands of places awaiting news, news of the utmost importance to them, news of their life or death.*
>
> *Through his mind a thousand memories seethed; odd thoughts he could no longer hold from his tired brain—the little group of children he had seen yesterday playing in the park. The contented smile of employees finishing a day of useful work. The sparrows chirping among themselves the latest gossip.*

Powerful horses straining at their loads in the brisk dawn. Hearty farmers tilling their land with loving care. Pleasant little noises along his favorite trout stream. He looked at the empty chairs—and thought how they looked like a jury of ghosts...

Suddenly the door opened. The broadcasting authority said: You are on the air, sir.

He roused himself, cleared his throat, and began his speech, a speech that could only end in bloodshed. His tired voice carried the black message into the night.

JOACHIM

Hitler responded to Britain's declaration of war with a speech delivered to Germany later that day, charging that Britain had started a war; he accused the English of attempting to encircle and weaken Germany, and he recalled for his countrymen Germany's ignominious submission at Versailles. He painted a picture of British aggression, against which it was their right to fight:

> *I had for years been aware that the aim of these war inciters had for long been to take Germany by surprise at a favorable opportunity. I am more firmly determined than ever to beat back this attack. Germany shall not again capitulate. There is no sense in sacrificing one life after another and submitting to an even worse Versailles Diktat. We have never been a nation of slaves and will not be one in the future. Whatever Germans in the past had to sacrifice for the existence of our realm, they shall not be greater than those, which we are today prepared to make.*

When the war started in September, Joachim's squadron, Jagdgeschwader 26, was not deployed over Poland, but was ordered to "defend the Ruhr region with is vital industries and guard the western front." The front, including the English Channel, was quiet, borders were to be respected, as was Belgian-Dutch neutrality. While there wasn't much action, his deployment gave Joachim valuable flying time as he learned every nuance of his fighter, a Messerschmitt Bf 109.

TED

Ted and the rest of the world had watched the catastrophe of Poland from afar. The newspaper headlines in the *Oakland Tribune* on September 2 trumpeted Britain's ultimatum that Germany withdraw from Poland. Acting in the same capacity he had in Munich the year before, Mussolini, still not formally allied with the Nazis, prepared a peace plan. On September 3, the entire front page of Ted's local metropolitan paper was about Poland, its citizens who had died in the Nazi invasion, the peace plan sent to Hitler, and the pending expiration of the Allied ultimatum. On September 4, a German U-boat (submarine) attacked a French ship and the following day Roosevelt signed a proclamation barring U.S. citizens from aiding any of the belligerents. On Wednesday, September 27, Ted learned that Warsaw was in flames and had surrendered.

JOACHIM

Pilots in general—even those at the center of action—do not witness carnage up close like the men on the ground do, but Joachim could not have missed the death notices that began to appear in the state-sanctioned paper. He likely scanned them for names of those he knew—the "fallen" who would live on in memory. On October 8, 1939, there was a whole page of paid notices in the paper. To make it easy for families, the newspaper provided a template with blanks that could easily be filled in with their loved one's name, date of death, and age: *"In a hero's death for Führer, Volk and Vaterland, there died ___ in the fighting in___ my beloved son, aged ___."*[44]

After two months of patrolling Germany's western borders, on November 7, 1939, southwest of Opladen, Joachim had his first victory: A Bristol Bleinheim I that had strayed into German territory. The plane was piloted by H.R. Bewley, flying with the RAF's 57th Squadron, who survived to become a Prisoner of War. For this first victory, sometimes called a "kill," Joachim was awarded the Iron Cross, Second Class. The telegram he received in recognition of his victory is pasted in his album in the center of a page surrounded by photographs of the wreckage, half buried in the earth where it fell. In Joachim's hand, the page is titled, "Der erste Abschuss!" The first shooting.

It took Germany just four weeks to conquer and divide Poland. Though its western Allies, Britain and France, were preparing for war, they never made it to the front, leaving the Poles to face Germany's "blitzkrieg" tactics alone. Bombs rained from the air and thousands of tanks rolled in, crushing tens of thousands of soldiers fighting on horseback. Valiant, but badly outmatched, having lost 120,000 men and another million captured, Poland surrendered on September 27.

Then, for months, there was, it seemed, no actual war going on. The Allies called this period the "phony war" and the Germans called it "sitzkrieg" (which literally means "sitting war"). The period from the autumn of 1939 when Germany battered Poland until May 1940 when they invaded France and the Low Countries was quiet. While not much happened on land, at sea the German Navy was actively pursuing and sinking British merchant vessels. Britain was sending troops and material to Norway, but for months, there was no apparent engagement as the Allies gave Germany just what they needed— time to repair, regroup, and begin building a national myth that the German military was invincible.

Ted

Ted titled the October 12, Cabbages and Kings column "War Worries" and in it he makes several cryptic observations about rationing in Germany and neutrality debates in the US; he glides lightly by Hitler's "Appeal for Peace" speech after decimating Warsaw by suggesting that Hitler looks like he might take up fireside chatting.

What is happening in Europe is clearly present in Ted's consciousness as he frequently alludes to world affairs in his column, but he also muses about every day pleasures and concerns of college life: lemon cokes on a hot autumn night or how a photographer can best position himself on the field to snap good photos at football games. He worked hard on a short story about death, which was published by the school's literary magazine, but Ted's story is about an imagined death of a single man. It's a far cry from the "Tale of Slaughter of Polish civilians" published October 6, 1939, in *Time,* a magazine that Ted read regularly.

As the "Phony War" persisted, however, life returned to normal and the headlines in metropolitan dailies used less ink. Having successfully completed another semester at college, Ted ended 1939 on an upbeat note. It's not quite up to Carroll's rhyme scheme, but the sentiment of his last column of the year is clear. Finals are over, Christmas is coming, and in his world, there is peace.

When Christmas comes,
The relatives too,
With gaudy ties of red, white and blue--
The kind the salesman pulls from under the
Counter with a leer
When kindly grandma ventures near.

The family gathers round a
Groaning table
We eat and eat and eat, then arise
If we are able.
Then out come the pipes and cigars,
With peaceful talk of happy men.

Then back to school, the
Same old grind
While we hope to all, the
World be kind.

From January 1939 through August 1940, Ted wrote a weekly, often satirical, column for the college newspaper, The Santa Clara.

Joachim scored his first victory on November 7, 1939. This page of his album entitled "The First Shot!" includes the telegram awarding him his first medal, the Iron Cross, 2nd class.

CHAPTER 11

Fight or Flight

———

The fateful year [1939] faded into history in a curious and even eerie
atmosphere. Though there was world war, there was no fighting
on land, and in the skies the big bombers carried only propaganda
pamphlets, and badly written ones at that. Only at sea was there
actual warfare. U-boats continued to take their toll of British and
sometimes neutral shipping in the cruel, icy northern Atlantic.[45]

WILLIAM L. SHIRER

TED

TED'S FIRST COLUMN OF THE new decade begins with a dirge for the thirties,

> *...a time of economic strife, poverty, experimentation; with political*
> *change, anxiety, and the too frequent abolishment of the Old Order; with*
> *militant storm clouds gathering and rushing at each other with appar-*
> *ently irresistible force—these comprise the tome which we will call the*
> *threatening thirties. It is ended.*

The past was bleak, but the future does not look so bright to Ted either: *with*
three good sized wars going on and the bystanders sharpening their swords, the val-
iant Finns fighting off the Russian monster, Japan cutting deep into China's heart,
and the Western Front temporarily frozen between a bloody war and real peace.
   War will come, he predicts, in spring:

With the Big Blowup, in which all great nations will become inextricably involved will come defeat, ruin, and isolation. This will act as a purge of some evil and some good, most purges are. ... The living will gather up the shattered pieces and try to remake the world in the same mold. It will fail. Then perhaps the world will be reformed to man in his present form of enlightenment—with a civilization suited to him, not as a machine but as an intellectual creature with untouched capabilities. Society will be founded upon that which is morally right, physically sound, and socially secure.

So far the world has seen fit to regard man as an animal, completely ignoring a world that constitutes fully half, the most important half—his spiritual side.

JOACHIM

In Joachim's world, the Nazis were taking full advantage of man's ability to learn to act like a machine. Fathers and sons were recruited to build a mechanized juggernaut with row upon row of round-helmeted, uniformed men who subordinated their individuality to the greater community of the Volk and the security of routine.

As members of a group, they didn't need to make hard choices or take responsibility for choices made for them. They had been taught to obey; they had been conditioned not to question authority. If they had any qualms about what they were asked to do, Joachim and his generation had learned to muffle their conscience; it was always better to be quiet. Anyway, they didn't have choices; they had only duty. The war into which they were marching was morally right and fair because the Führer said so and, as the propaganda had taught them day in and day out since they were children: "Der Führer Hat Immer Recht" (The Leader is Always Right).

From our vantage point in the twenty-first century, we can see WWII for all its horror, but at the time Hitler had two very different objectives: one was territorial expansion and the other was to exterminate Jews. While these objectives were overt, some scholars say it was possible that the German "people identified the war, not with the Nazi regime, but with their own intergenerational familial responsibilities. It was the strongest foundation for their patriotism."[46] It's possible to believe that Joachim fought to redeem the failure of his father's war. It's possible to imagine that he believed he was fighting a war for a just and righteous cause as it redressed the grievances of his father, and his father's generation.

Joachim was also, however, clearly fighting for Hitler as he, like every member of the military, had sworn allegiance not to Germany, not to the German people, but to Adolf Hitler, the man, their leader, der Führer.

> *I swear by God this sacred oath that to the Leader of the German empire and people, Adolf Hitler, supreme commander of the armed forces, I shall render unconditional obedience and that as a brave soldier I shall at all times be prepared to give my life for this oath.*

If someone chooses to fight for a particular leader, are they not complicit in achieving the goals established by that leadership? Official records indicate that, like over half of the German population at the time, Joachim was not a member of the Nazi party and there are no pictures of him with his arm outstretched, hailing an invisible but omnipresent Hitler though he no doubt did so in public. It's equally clear he was enthusiastic about his job; he liked what he was doing. In 1940, he was called to make good on the pledge he had made to the Führer and he did. In fact, his victories would earn him glory, fame, and recognition by the Führer himself.

TED

In the spring of 1940, while Germany was strategically occupying Norway and Denmark and Joachim was climbing into the cockpit of his Messerschmitt to fight over Belgium, the Netherlands and France, Ted was studying for final exams, but his grades were falling and he wondered what he was doing with his life. Studying English literature seemed so trivial, so selfish. What was the point? In his newspaper column, he had begun to question the purpose of education in a series of Platonic dialogues with a troll named Nug.

Might education be a pencil sharpener? ... I mean an institution to sharpen the ego in order to write upon the book of life a few words or perhaps even a page?

No that is too definite, it is something less positive...

Could education be a river bed over which the stream of life may flow, passing over rocks and under low hanging branches?

It could be, but that suggests a predetermined course. Education leaves a greater selection.

Then it is more of a handbook of mathematical tables and formulas, a foundation from which we adduce those formulas and put them to work.

You are getting somewhere now...Perhaps it is a road map that shows us different courses of action, and yet leaves us to choose any road we wish.

But why should one get an education or is it necessary?

Nug replied: It is the only way to begin to solve the problem that we all have. It is the first step in living, the first rung in the ladder leading to the mesa we call happiness.

Do you mean that it is confined to book learning, or is there some other way that it may be obtained?

Yes, it may be obtained from just living, but it is far more difficult. There are so many obstacles and apparent contradictions that we meet, many of which are isolated from institutions of learning. ...

As the world order shifted in Europe, Ted's world—one of safety, deliberation, wonder, and discussion seemed increasingly irrelevant. He was no longer happy in his studies, but at the same time, he reasoned that the purpose of education, ultimately, was to bring happiness.

What is happiness, Nug? Is it the jingling of a bell?

For some it is—a reaching for something they will never get, a striving for something they will never attain.

Is it a pomegranate to be eaten delicately and the unwanted rind to be thrown away?

That is more nearly correct—a choosing of the useful and beneficial and a disregarding of the waste.

For others is it a dream to be cherished, but never achieved, a sort of nightmare?

No; more exactly it is a goal, the mesa from which we may view the heavens unobstructed.

Then happiness should be a norm for which we may strive as a means to an end, the end being something that has no material existence?

Yes, true happiness is a norm, but as in everything else there are many false values to be judged and chosen or disregarded, which we may say is the purpose of education.

Ted was carrying on this conversation in print, with a fictitious troll, but it wasn't long before it became evident that Ted wondered why he was in school at all. Two months before Germany made the move on the Low Countries, Ted speculated that Germany would march on the Netherlands, triggering Japan's capture of the Dutch East Indies, the source of ninety percent of America's rubber. His column ends with a caution: "We must bear in mind that this is not the second war of Germany against England and France, it is the second World War and conditions such as these should not be ignored."

JOACHIM

On May 10, 1940, the "Phony War" ended as, true to Ted's prediction, the Nazis invaded France, Belgium, Luxembourg and the Netherlands, and Neville Chamberlain, the Prime Minister who had spear-headed appeasement, stepped down to a round of parliament's appreciative applause. On May 10, with little fanfare and less enthusiasm from his colleagues in parliament, Winston Churchill became the new Prime Minister of Britain.

On May 11, Joachim scored his second victory: A French Curtiss Hawk northeast of Antwerp, Belgium. The following week, as the Germans pushed towards France, he flew south and west past Brussels to Ath, shooting down two RAF Hurricanes, and fatally wounding Sgt. J.L.C. Williams.

On May 13, 1940, Winston Churchill addressed members of the House of Commons, and the people of Britain, the United Kingdom, and the New World. As they took up the task of fighting for England—and to achieve victory for democracy over tyranny. He had nothing to offer, he said, "but blood, toil, tears and sweat."

We have before us an ordeal of the most grievous kind. We have before us many, many long months of struggle and of suffering. You ask, what is our policy? I can say: It is to wage war, by sea, land and air, with all our might and with all the strength that God can give us; to wage war against a monstrous tyranny, never surpassed in the dark, lamentable catalogue of human crime. That is our policy. You ask, what is our aim?

I can answer in one word: It is victory, victory at all costs, victory in spite of all terror, victory, however long and hard the road may be; for without victory, there is no survival. Let that be realized; no survival for the British Empire, no survival for all that the British Empire has stood for, no survival for the urge and impulse of the ages, that mankind will move forward towards its goal. But I take up my task with buoyancy and hope. I feel sure that our cause will not be suffered to fail among men. At this time, I feel entitled to claim the aid of all, and I say, "come then, let us go forward together with our united strength.

TED

The spring semester was over and Ted had some time with his family and friends. With the invasion of France and the Low Countries, war worries were escalating; the United States had not joined its allies in a declaration of war, but Roosevelt was asking for appropriations to fund the expansion of the military—especially airplanes. Ted was subdued. It was summertime; two years before he had enjoyed a carefree summer in a Europe that was being hammered by a despot. America was an ocean away, and was not in the war, but somehow he felt that it was his duty to do something. On Sunday, May 26, he joined his father in his study to listen to Roosevelt's "fireside chat" on the subject of national defense.

Tonight over the once peaceful roads of Belgium and France millions are now moving, running from their homes to escape bombs and shells and fire and machine gunning, without shelter, and almost wholly without food. They stumble on, knowing not where the end of the road will be.

America, FDR said, could not be isolated; the American military was strong and growing stronger; American industrial strength was only just being tapped.

They turned off the radio and for a while, father and son talked about their memories of those very roads in France and about what America could do. Ernest was most eager to talk about America's industrial strength. Roosevelt was right, he said, it was as yet untapped. He told Ted about visiting ship-building plants in the area. Henry Kaiser was a neighbor and friend and Ernest talked to him about how they might be able improve production and reduce labor costs by using giant magnets instead of manpower to move the metal pieces. He was, he told Ted, working on an idea. He opened his notebook, dated a page and started to sketch it out, talking about how the magnets could be manipulated mechanically, infinitely increasing each man's strength.

Ted listened to his father, always the businessman. Always thinking of ways to make things work better, ways to make money. He nodded at the drawing and wondered aloud if, perhaps, he should enlist. He had always wanted to fly, he said, perhaps he could join the Army Air Corps. He wasn't doing much at school—not anything he felt he could be proud of.

Ernest put his pencil down and leaned back in his chair. FDR's speech had made him think about industry, efficiency, ingenuity—all the ways America needed to work better, faster, more productively. His twenty-year old son had heard that America was readying itself for war; already Roosevelt said the Army was twice what it had been. Roosevelt's speech had made Ted think about the many men that would be needed. He talked about dropping out of college and joining the army.

They talked long into the night. In the end, they both agreed that, for now, Ted should finish his final year and his degree in English, a worthy pursuit and preparation for almost any career. Neither knew what that would be, but they were both sure that whatever came, there would be opportunities.

JOACHIM

In Europe, war was raging. Germany had trampled over Belgium and the Netherlands and fighting raged deep into France as the Germans beat the

Allies back to the western edge of the continent, where thousands of British and French soldiers were stranded.

The day after Roosevelt's fireside chat, using the name "Operation Dynamo," a ragtag navy from Britain began evacuating nearly 340,000 French and British soldiers from the beaches at Dunkirk. Joachim was in the air over the channel, where he doubled his kill scorecard, a feat that would earn for him a second medal, this time an Iron Cross, First Class.

At Dunkirk, Churchill feared that "the whole root and core and brain of the British Army had been stranded to perish or be captured." Dunkirk was a debacle that turned into a miracle for the Allies partly because, for some inexplicable reason, the Germans arrested their advance on the ground, though Joachim and his fellow fighter pilots did not stop strafing from above. For nine days and nights a motley flotilla of over 800 boats including fishing vessels, fire ships, paddle steamers, private yachts, motorboats, barges and lifeboats of every size and shape ferried exhausted troops, across the Channel.[47]

Above them, the Luftwaffe hunted; Joachim alone shot down six RAF planes: one Lysander, two Hurricanes and three Spitfires. It was the first battle in which the intrepid and nimble British Spitfires joined the fight with thirty-two RAF squadrons taking turns flying watches of forty minutes each, attempting to shield the men who had been pushed to the sea.

The beach, black with men, illumined by the fires, seemed a perfect target, but no doubt the thick clouds of smoke were a useful screen. The picture will always remain sharp-etched in my memory—the lines of men wearily and sleepily staggering across the beach from the dunes to the shallows, falling into little boats, great columns of men thrust out into the water among bomb and shell splashes. The foremost ranks were shoulder deep, moving forward under the command of young subalterns, themselves with their heads just above the little waves that rode in to the sand. As the front ranks were dragged aboard the boats, the rear ranks moved up, from ankle deep to knee deep, from knee deep to waist deep, until they, too, came to shoulder depth and their turn.

The little boats that ferried from the beach to the big ships in deep water listed drunkenly with the weight of men. The big ships slowly took on lists of their own with the enormous numbers crowded aboard. And always down the dunes and across the beach came new hordes of men, new columns, new lines.[48]

Not all the men waiting on the beach to be rescued made it to safety; nor did all of the pilots flying to protect them. But in the end, despite all odds, and protected by 40,000 French troops who fought until they ran out of ammunition, and were killed or captured, nearly all of the 340,000 Allied troops were ferried from the beach in France to safe haven in England. For ten long days and nights sheer will, heroism and discipline prevailed. Hitler might have taken note; the Allies were not likely to give up even if the odds were stacked mightily against them.

Ted

Two weeks before Ted's twenty-first birthday, "Operation Dynamo" was over and the boys who landed on the beaches at Dover were, to their amazement, heralded as heroes. They knew what they had seen, and they knew they had not returned in victory, but in abject defeat. A new, unwelcome war had begun and morale in Britain was low, but the indomitable Brits would not saddle their boys with the weight of their disappointment; they had done all they could and they would live to fight another day. Belgium and the Netherlands had both surrendered and the French were retreating. It was to this audience that Winston Churchill spoke on June 4, 1940, when he reported the valor of the operation and the defeat that had preceded it.

Even though large tracts of Europe and many old and famous States have fallen or may fall into the grip of the Gestapo and all the odious apparatus of Nazi rule, we shall not flag or fail.
We shall go on to the end, we shall fight in France,
we shall fight on the seas and oceans,
we shall fight with growing confidence and growing strength in the air, we shall defend our Island, whatever the cost may be,

we shall fight on the beaches,
we shall fight on the landing grounds,
we shall fight in the fields and in the streets,
we shall fight in the hills;

   we shall never surrender, and even if, which I do not for a moment
believe, this Island or a large part of it were subjugated and starving, then
our Empire beyond the seas, armed and guarded by the British Fleet,
would carry on the struggle, until, in God's good time, the New World,
with all its power and might, steps forth to the rescue and the liberation
of the old."

   Ten days later, the Nazis entered Paris. The Battle of France was over and most of Europe was occupied. Only Britain remained. On June 18, Churchill again addressed Parliament.

   What General Weygand has called the Battle of France is over ... the
Battle of Britain is about to begin. Upon this battle depends the survival
of Christian civilization. Upon it depends our own British life, and the
long continuity of our institutions and our Empire. The whole fury and
might of the enemy must very soon be turned on us. Hitler knows that he
will have to break us in this island or lose the war. If we can stand up to
him, all Europe may be freed and the life of the world may move forward
into broad, sunlit uplands.

   But if we fail, then the whole world, including the United States,
including all that we have known and cared for, will sink into the abyss of
a new dark age made more sinister, and perhaps more protracted, by the
lights of perverted science. Let us therefore brace ourselves to our duties, and
so bear ourselves, that if the British Empire and its Commonwealth last
for a thousand years, men will still say, This was their finest hour.[49]

They were his age, Ted knew, those men who were fighting; their lives had purpose. Three days after Churchill's speech, on June 21, 1940, in the forest of Compiegne, in the same place and the same rail car where the Armistice ending WWI had been signed, France surrendered to Germany. The symbolism was inescapable: the defeat of the previous war had been reversed.

Joachim

In Germany, *Signal,* the International Nazi Propaganda magazine, began publishing in April, 1940, and gave the German people photographs of men at war and graphics showing arrows of occupation. Propaganda extolled the virtues and amplified the successes of the German military, giving the people at home visual proof of the victories they should celebrate. The conquest of Poland had been, as planned, a quick and decisive "blitzkrieg" and while the subsequent months appeared to be a quiet "sitting war," Hitler had continued moving across the board of Europe, attacking neutral Denmark and Norway to secure the route that the iron ore from Sweden had to take to support the Third Reich.

By the end of May, with the Low Countries and Norway occupied, Germany could turn its attention to Britain. The goal was to sufficiently weaken the Royal Air Force and coastal shipping to make the planned invasion by land ("Operation Sea Lion") feasible.

Beginning on July 10, Joachim was one of the hundreds of fighters and bombers screaming over the Channel and the coast of England. Joachim, who had been promoted from Second Lieutenant to First Lieutenant for exceptional achievements, circled London, battered defending pilots on the coast, and harried ships, adding fifteen planes to his list of victories over Dover, Margate, Folkestone, Ashford, Braintree, Goodhurst, Maidstone, Faversham, and Marden. By August, the Luftwaffe had stepped up their attacks, sending a thousand planes a day over the channel. Joachim and JG 26 flew every day, relentlessly pummeling the RAF, and cratering the airfields. The strategy nearly worked.

Ted

In the summer of 1940, at home in California, Ted felt empty. Dull. His life was easy. Too easy. It was meaningless, really. He read *Time* magazine weekly and the paper daily, almost obsessively. He went on vacation with his family to their home at Lake Tahoe where he camped, fished, and water skied on the deep blue lake, clear as glass framed by the Sierra Nevada still snow-capped in mid-summer. He was alive and there was much for which he was thankful, but the lessons he had learned in his philosophy classes at Santa Clara gnawed at him. He was an opportunist floating with the tide, wandering without direction. He was not directing his life; he was simply living as a child does—without obligation or responsibility.

On August 13, the front page of the Oakland Tribune shouted: *Air Blitz Rages on 200-Mile Front. A riptide of Nazi aerial might, the third in three days, thundered across the staunchly defended coasts of England today.* The Germans were striking at British railroads and airports and propaganda from Berlin asserted that the German Air Force had control over Dover.

In his column for the school paper, dated August 22, 1940, Ted wrote:

Santa Clara has been out for three months...While we have been doing other things... Hitler has taken Norway, with a highly mechanized Trojan horse. He slashed through the Lowlands like a knife through melted butter. England thought it time to prepare while France thought it time to repair.

Two days later, on August 24, a couple of Luftwaffe bombers hit London's financial district, Oxford Street and the West End where Ted had walked with his brother two summers before. As Hitler had expressly directed that central London should not be attacked, the target was probably not intentional, but Churchill did not wait for an explanation, which he would not have believed anyway, and immediately ordered a retaliatory strike.

On August 25, 1940, seventy RAF planes were sent to Berlin. No one was killed on the ground and despite the "magnificent and terrible sight"[50] of the anti-aircraft fire, no plane was brought down either. But for the Germans, who had been repeatedly promised that enemy planes could not penetrate the anti-aircraft defense rings circling the city, the specter of British aircraft over Germany, the shrieking sirens, the pounding of guns and the bombs exploding brought war home. Goering who had promised it could never happen was embarrassed. Hitler was livid.

Bombing Berlin turned out to be successful in a way Churchill could not have foreseen: it triggered Hitler's ire and he changed his strategy. Unbeknownst to him, the strategic bombing of British military installations had almost completely disabled the RAF, but after Berlin was bombed, he redirected the Luftwaffe to "terror bomb" London.

The English did not buckle in terror, the RAF had a chance to rebuild, and in California, thousands of miles away from the escalating war, Ted could no longer justify to himself what he was doing with his life. He had struck a light tone in his column two days earlier, but he couldn't keep it up. Just after the bombs fell on London's West End, Ted was still unsure about what direction he would take with his life, but he knew that for now at least, it was not to pursue a degree in English. He wrote his last column and dropped out of college. He would not return except as a name stamped in high relief on a bronze plaque in the chapel, one of Santa Clara's fallen.

JOACHIM

Nearly the same day that Ted dropped out of college, on August 22, Joachim was promoted to Captain of 7 Squadron, JG 26. Two weeks later, he was one of the 648 fliers supporting 625 bombers raining havoc on London. For fifty-seven nights beginning on September 7, 1940 ("Black Saturday"), the Luftwaffe, blitzed Britain's capital city. By the time Hitler suspended the assault, Joachim had scored twenty-two victories in and around London and, around his neck, the coveted Knight's Cross dangled.

Despite massive effort, Germany failed to invade Britain. Nearly all of the continent had fallen to the Nazis, but even with no Allies to support them and the US still claiming neutrality, Britain would not buckle. On September 20, Hitler permanently postponed landing on the British Isles. A few weeks later, Joachim scored his twenty-third victory over the English Channel, a Spitfire from the RAF's 74th squadron on the coast near Dover.

Joachim returned to Germany for a few weeks leave, giving him some time for relaxation and a hero's welcome. The October edition of *Luftflotte West* featured Joachim in a double spread of photos, some of which were made into postcards—a happy, handsome face of a twenty-one-year-old war hero.

TED

Ted's decision to drop out of college in the fall of what would have been his final year caused a bit of a row with his father. Ted knew his dad loved him, but Ernest made it clear that he thought that his son was behaving badly. Spoiled. As if the world owed him a living. Ted didn't think the world owed him anything, but he wasn't at all sure what he owed the world. He knew he didn't want to go into business like his older brothers. And he couldn't sit in classrooms anymore talking about what a lot of dead people had thought about a world that didn't exist anymore. It just seemed so useless. Ernest Hemingway was one of his favorite authors and he had never gone to college. He didn't need to go to college to be a writer or a photographer.

Anyway, he didn't know what he wanted when he dropped out of school, but his father was clear: If he wasn't going to school he needed to get a job and pay his own way.

In fall of 1940, Ted sailed to Hawaii, went to work as a photographer for the Eastman Kodak Company, got himself an efficiency apartment, and went out most evenings to join the crowd mingling on Hotel Street, often packed with sailors stationed at nearby Pearl Harbor. The boys wearing the starched whites of the US Navy were mostly Ted's age.

When Ted got together with his sailor friends, they talked about war. They hoped it would start soon because they didn't want to miss it. They had had enough spit and polish and making their bunk so tight an officer could bounce a quarter off it. A war would be a chance for them to be someone. Ted, too, had been thinking a lot about war. Not long before he sailed to Hawaii, he met a WWI veteran who had lost an arm. Ted bought him coffee and they talked for a while and later he wrote a short piece of fiction that featured a veteran's memories:

The sting of burning flesh; the stink of rotting bodies; the scream of despairing women; the cursing of soldiers; the death-whistle of bombs; the lisp of crickets in a momentary lull. Beseeching limbs of charred trees; the empty arms of mothers. The rattle of fixed bayonets; the tinkle of surgeon's tools. Clenched fists; huddled babies; shattered buildings; broken men. All, all useless, hopeless, terrible...

Ted called the piece "Pax Vobiscum" (Peace be with you) the Latin greeting Catholics share at mass. Later, in Hawaii, he felt much older than he had been when he wrote it. His father had been right – independence was a good teacher. Being in Hawaii where young Americans were gathering to serve had brought the war in the Pacific a whole lot closer than it had been when he had stood at the microphone hosting debates about whether or not conflicts in Europe and Asia were America's problem.

JOACHIM

With the attack on Britain suspended, Joachim was sent to Sicily from where he continued the assault on Malta that had begun the previous June. Despite relentless attacks, the island nation refused to surrender and remained a thorn in the side of the Axis as its strategic location gave the Allies a base from which to attack German and Italian ships on their way to supplying troops in North Africa.

Malta is tiny, but it was an indomitable fortress. In the next months, and years, Joachim would fly scores of sorties, and shoot down dozens of planes from this Allied safe haven. For his efforts, he was the first foreigner to be awarded the Italian Gold Medal for Bravery.[51] It was prestigious recognition for the role Joachim and JG 26, played in supporting the Axis powers as they relentlessly attempted to deal a knockout blow to the island.

TED

Ted, too, was on an island, a much bigger one that would soon play an important role in America's eventual decision to go to war. He had been in Hawaii four months when on December 29, 1940, he tuned into Roosevelt's fireside chat as FDR warned the nation about the pact that Germany, Italy, and Japan had signed, signaling their solidarity and their belligerence. Ted knew that, 2500 miles away, his father would be listening to the same broadcast:

Never before since Jamestown and Plymouth Rock has our American civilization been in such danger as now. For, on September 27, 1940, by an agreement signed in Berlin, three powerful nations, two in Europe and one in Asia, joined themselves together in the threat that if the United States of America interfered with or blocked the expansion program of these three nations—a program aimed at world control—they would unite in ultimate action against the United States. The Nazi masters of Germany have made it clear that they intend not only to dominate all life and thought in their own country, but also to enslave the whole of Europe, and then to use the resources of Europe to dominate the rest of the world. It was only three weeks ago their leader stated this: "There are two worlds that stand opposed to each other." And then in defiant reply to his opponents, he said this: "Others are correct when they say: With this world we cannot ever reconcile ourselves…. I can beat any other power in the world." So said the leader of the Nazis.

Roosevelt countered the isolationist argument with the statement: *Even today we have planes that could fly from the British Isles to New England and back again without refueling.* Britain was fighting for the free world and it was, he believed, the free world's obligation to assist.

Over the next few months, Ted continued to work at the Eastman Kodak Company. He wrote in his journal; he attempted to write short stories; and he wrote long letters to his friend, Bill, who agreed with Roosevelt. America should not stand by and neither, he thought, should they.

As the Battle of Britain raged from mid-July to September, 1940, Joachim tallied nearly twenty victories, was promoted to Captain and awarded the Knight's Cross.

At Santa Clara, Ted hosted radio debates about American involvement in the war.

Part Four:
Worlds Collide 1941 – 1943

CHAPTER 12

From the Pacific to the Mediterranean

―――

THE YEAR 1941 WOULD BE a turning point in the war. At the beginning of the year, nineteen-year-old Mavis Lever, working at Britain's Bletchley Park, cracked the Italian Navy's code: It was the same one they had used during the Spanish Civil War. The first message, "Today's the day, minus three" was followed by a second informing the British that an Italian fleet was preparing to attack near Cape Matapan in the eastern Mediterranean. The British already had the advantage of radar, and Mavis had given them another: They could listen in as the Italian ships took their positions.

The second game-changer was Japan bombing Pearl Harbor and Hitler's subsequent declaration of war on Japan's enemy, the United States. Both events would turn the tide against a still belligerent Germany, which had neither the manpower nor the resources to succeed in what had become a war of attrition.

JOACHIM

In 1940, Joachim had participated in the invasion of France and the Battle of Britain and he had well earned a home leave that enabled him to be present at his childhood home in Friedrichshof for the wedding of his sister, Eva-Brigitte, to his best friend, Heinz Hoffstätter.

In February 1941, Joachim returned to duty in the Mediterranean, which the Italians called "Mare Nostrum" (our sea). This time his orders were to neutralize Malta at all costs, and he went right to work, downing one Wellington, one Spitfire, and eight Hurricanes.

On March 28, as the sun set, he took off from Gela, Sicily to fly his two-hundredth combat mission and score his thirty-third kill. Joachim's downed Hurricane from the RAF's 261 squadron was a small victory on a day that, with the tactical advantage provided by Bletchley Park, the British navy was laying claim to the Italian Sea.

Joachim was seven hours' flying time from the cape where the fate of the Mediterranean was being played out, as British and Italian battleships, destroyers, and light and heavy cruisers engaged in an intricate tango. Both fleets misidentified opponents, zigzagged, reversed, pursued, laid smoke, and sped up to evade white frothed torpedoes aimed at their vulnerable underbellies. By nightfall on March 28, with the ability to decode their messages and superior firepower, the British triumphed, losing one aircraft, but crippling and sinking four Italian destroyers and three heavy cruisers. The Mediterranean was, temporarily at least, no longer Italy's "Mare Nostrum." The following week Joachim and his squadron were ordered to fly north to subdue the Balkans.

TED

For Ted, it was difficult to reconcile his idyllic memories of Europe with the specter of the war ravaging the countryside, crushing buildings, extinguishing the lives of so many young men like him and those he had met at Pearl Harbor. In the summer of 1938, he had driven into Paris the day after Queen Elizabeth and King George VI had arrived on their grand tour of peace and goodwill. Crowds wearing the red, white and blue of both countries' flags had gathered along the wide boulevards of Paris to cheer the young monarchs, parading the solidarity of democracy to the rest of the world. Ted, too, had walked the long Avenue des Champs-Élysées past the Arc de Triomphe, pausing at the Tomb of the Unknown Soldier with his brother, cameras dangling around their necks. Those streets were now filled with German soldiers who also carried cameras, nestled next to their guns, taking snapshots of the city they had conquered.[52] London, too, continued to be under siege.

Thousands of miles away from the fighting in Europe, Ted cheered on March 11, 1941, when the Lend-Lease Act passed over the opposition—at least America could do something as the president now had authority to provide arms and war materials to "the government of any country whose defense the President deems vital to the defense of the United States." Britain and the Soviet Union were immediate beneficiaries.

In April, Yugoslavia unconditionally surrendered, and Greece fell under the Axis heel. With the Europe he had toured almost entirely consumed by Hitler's massive appetite, Ted quit his job, bought a third-class ticket on the *S.S. Mariposa Voy*, sailed to California, and on April 26, 1941, he enlisted in the United States Army. His best friend, Bill Gallagher, volunteered too, but Bill, it turned out, was not acceptable material for the United States Armed Forces. Ernest Hemingway, one of Ted's heroes, could not serve in WWI because of his eyesight. Bill was fit, well-educated, and his eyesight was just fine; he was a patriot, and he was gay.

JOACHIM

Joachim had joined in the conquest of Yugoslavia that had begun on April 6. Battered by the onslaught of ground troops and the Luftwaffe, it wasn't long before the Balkan state was dissolved, renamed Montenegro and shoved under the protectionist umbrella of Nazi Germany's ally, Fascist Italy. After a brief stint over Belgrade, Joachim was ordered back to Malta.

On May 7, having scored forty-three victories, Joachim became the twelfth recipient of the Oak Leaves to add to his Knight's Cross. As his biographer wrote, "The Messerschmitt with the yellow nose, the red heart, and the number 12 was now equally famous and feared."[53]

In the spring of 1941, the war was spreading like wildfire and the wind was blowing mostly, but not completely, in Germany's favor. The British had gained some control of the Mediterranean, and despite thousands of tons of bombs, Malta continued to offer stiff resistance to the Nazi attempt to conquer it. Erwin Rommel, the commander of the German troops in North Africa (Afrika Korps), was on the attack, but his success was heavily dependent on supply convoys navigating the Mediterranean, which no longer had the protection of much of the Italian fleet.

Yugoslavia had officially fallen, though guerrilla resistance continued and there were other setbacks for the Germans like the British sinking of the pride of their fleet, the "unsinkable" battleship *Bismarck* in the North Atlantic. The battle in the Mediterranean was far from over, but the Axis powers had lost their undisputed supremacy and their beachheads in North Africa were at risk as supply convoys couldn't get through.

Still, propaganda ensured that on the home front, it appeared that all was well as the Allies had suffered a series of humiliating defeats, which Germany's state-controlled media could exaggerate and celebrate. For his part, Hitler thought he knew the Allied leaders who had, two years earlier, meekly exchanged the Sudetenland for a promise he had never intended to keep. If they had the stomach to fight at all, he was sure it wouldn't be for long. The Germans were making their way steadily across Egypt towards the Suez Canal, where they could sever Britain's access to India.

The next step according to Hitler's plan was to start as early as possible after the spring thaw to break the Nonaggression Pact he had made with Stalin two years earlier. After Germany attacked their erstwhile allies with a massive blitzkrieg, the Communists from Russia would no longer pose a threat and Hitler reasoned that the British would surely be ready to negotiate for peace in the west. He was proved wrong on both counts: The Soviet Union did not surrender and Britain never cut a deal that would, Churchill argued, undermine the very foundation of democracy.

TED

In June 1941, as the German army, supported by the Luftwaffe, crossed into the Soviet Union, Ted hunkered down and studied to become a pilot. Assigned to the Mira Loma Army base planted in the middle of lima bean and sugar beet farms in Oxnard, California, he thought he had never studied so hard. He had made the cut—the first one—but there was a long road to the Air Force. He and Bill Gallagher had had many talks about when war is justifiable and when serving the country—even if it means killing people—is the right thing to do. They talked about life as an adventure, but also as an obligation. They talked about how German men their age justified to themselves the war they had started.

After Bill was rejected by the armed forces because of his sexual orientation, he and Ted spent many hours talking about what it means to be free—to say what you think and to be who you are. Ted had long known that Bill wasn't interested in women, but it didn't make their friendship any different.

Ted loved the feel of women, their softness, their differentness; he knew he wasn't gay, but he loved Bill, too. Bill was the most important friend he had. They could talk about anything—hopes and fears and love; religion and death and the meaning of life. They were both deeply Catholic. They had both been taught that homosexuality was not part of God's plan.

It's not clear how they resolved who Bill knew himself to be with what their church was teaching. It is clear that they remained deeply committed to one another and to their church. For his part, though he had hoped to join with his friend, Ted was still eager to serve, but he knew that his previous experiences in college, boxing, football, writing, photography and backpacking did not prepare him for flying. He wanted to be in the pilot's seat, but he'd never been in an airplane. The highest he'd ever been was still on the ground—the 10,000-foot summit of Lake Tahoe's Mount Tallac—and the closest he'd ever been to an airplane was in the movie theater with Errol Flynn. But there was a brand new wing of the Army: The United States Army Air Force and that's the outfit he set his sights on joining. He knew it would be competitive; there were a lot of young men who had a lot more experience than he did. In his letter to his parents, he described his disadvantage:

> *I spent the weekend around the post, only leaving it to attend Mass this morning. Most of the time I spent studying and trying to keep up my navigation course, it's quite difficult especially as most of the fellows here have had primary training in C.A.A. [Civil Aeronautics Administration] and have had all these courses and flying before. It certainly keeps me stepping both on the ground and in the air to keep up with them. When a fellow has had around sixty hours of flying he has quite an advantage over one that has never been taught what the rudder pedals are used for, which happens to be my case.*

JOACHIM

Not long after Joachim was awarded the Oak Leaves, Joachim's commanding officer, Adolf Galland, received the Swords, beating Joachim's medal tally by one. Joachim wrote to him, ostensibly to congratulate him for the recognition, but the real intent of Joachim's congratulatory letter was likely self-promotion. Joachim apparently suffered from what the Germans called "Halsweh," which literally means sore throat, but the word was used as a metaphor for ambition.[54] Someone with a sore throat was always angling for more medals to adorn their sore neckline and Joachim was eager to add swords to his neckline, as his friend Galland had.

> *Esteemed Herr Obersleutnant! … It was with endless and proud joy that we learned yesterday of our Geschewader's great successes and the first-time awarding of the Oak Leaves with Swords to the Herr Obersleutnant.…*
>
> *…My fears of going stale in Greece were, thank God, not entirely founded. After about 14 days of rest in Catania I moved to the south Peloponnese. It is truly desolate in the Peloponnese. Unbelievable heat, much dust, life in tents, and all the while cut off from the outside world. Tactical employment is correspondingly meager, engaging sea targets in the eastern Mediterranean in cooperation with a Stuka-Gruppe. This required us to fly marine reconnaissance once or twice daily with long-range tanks up to 200 kilometers south of Crete. Two and half to three hours flying time, of course without any results, as the English fleet is sufficiently tied up in Syria. As well the whole thing was carried out with no air-sea rescue service, and was therefore not very pleasant.*
>
> *…Obedient thanks by the way for the transfer of Obit. Lindemann. I haven't seen him yet because he is always flying behind me. Sitting way out here, one sometimes gets homesick for one's old unit, but feelings must not determine actions at the front. I would only ask, Herr Oberstleutnant, that you not forget us…*[55]

The day after Galland's award on June 22, 1941, Hitler launched his long-planned invasion of the Soviet Union, code named "Operation Barbarossa." Joachim was not on the Eastern Front at the beginning, but three thousand tanks, 150 divisions, and three million German soldiers advanced. Joachim's father, Major Paul Müncheberg, was among them, leading a convoy of over 1000 men and 1300 horses over sandy roads that were often nearly impassable.

While his father was in Russia, Joachim was deployed to North Africa where for two years Axis and Allied forces had been chasing each other. The British and Commonwealth troops held on to Egypt and the Suez Canal; Libya and Tunisia were controlled by Germany. Joachim was in Tobruk, Libya, where the heat was oppressive, and they were outnumbered by the enemy three to one. On July 15, as the sultry afternoon melted into evening, he engaged with a swarm of RAF Hurricanes. Though he was not sure whether it was a pilot from the 73rd or the 229th squadron, he wrote that he was "unpleasantly chased…I soon had my revenge and sent a Curtiss down like a blazing torch into the sand." [56]

The following month, on July 29, Joachim downed a Hurricane and a P-40 in quick succession, then flew back to base, wagging the wings of his plane, known as "White 12", as was customary, to signal a confirmed victory. In his biography of Joachim, Hans-Joachim Röll recorded a story that reveals how his men felt about their leader.

While the other pilots chatted lively over the radio, Müncheberg remained quiet. Leaning forward slightly, he steered his Messerschmitt towards the paved coastal road. A convoy of trucks that had just stopped could be seen below them. The drivers jumped out of their cabs and waved up to the fighters. The planes returned the greeting amicably by rocking their wings.

Shortly afterwards, Müncheberg saw the familiar oval of the airfield with the low huts, the tents around the border and the benzene barrels filled with sand that served as splitter boxes for the machines. The other Me's made space for the White 12 as though by secret arrangement. Moments later, Müncheberg began the act that would repeat itself often in the coming month: He swept over the area at a low altitude. The wing tips alternately waving towards the ground. At the other side of the border, he shot like an arrow back into the sky, came back after turning and targeted the runway anew. The wings moved again as a sign for the second aerial victory.

> *At the mooring, the control room joyously threw their pith helmets in the air. Müncheberg extended the landing gear and landed gently. The Me rolled out dragging a long cloud of dust behind it and chugged to the mooring. Already from afar, he recognized the lean figure of the commander [Major Eduard Neumann] among the ground personnel. Müncheberg stopped his machine at its parking spot, turned off the engine and pushed the cabin cover to the side. Impatiently, he fumbled to undo the seatbelt and climbed out onto the wing where he paused with weak knees.*
>
> *Meanwhile the men stormed around and dragged Müncheberg from the wing. Next to him the face of his look-out, Ludwig Haaf, appeared. He was beside himself with joy.*
>
> *"Man, Mr. First Lieutenant!" he shouted, "two downed planes again! Is this possible?"*
>
> *Müncheberg gulped and nodded to his mechanic, much too exhausted for a fitting response. Suddenly, "Edu" Neumann [his commanding officer] appeared out of nowhere. Silence immediately fell. The captain shook Müncheberg's hand heartily. His gaze flitted over the sweat-drenched face that could only manage a feeble smile:*
>
> *"Müncheberg, I congratulate you!"*[57]

With a total of forty-eight victories, Joachim was redeployed again, this time back to France and the Western Front. It was August, and as Joachim began to record another series of victories over England and the Channel, Roosevelt and Churchill were meeting off the coast of Newfoundland. There was not much in the way of a formal binding commitment in what would become known as "The Atlantic Charter," but Hitler was on notice: the US would not abandon what had once been her mother country.

Germany, however, continued its assault and the RAF pilots on the western front continued to be battered with Joachim adding his expertise. The Messerschmitt with the red-heart on its fuselage was on the hunt and Joachim recorded victories from Abbeville to Boulogne, from Margate to Maidstone. Before the end of the year, over twenty RAF fliers would fall to his guns—all but one a Spitfire and his total scorecard of confirmed kills climbed to over sixty.

TED

In August 1941, as Joachim was scoring his fiftieth kill ten kilometers north of Dunkirk, Ted passed his twenty-hour check, which he noted was another milestone on his long road to wings of silver. He was now an aviation cadet, stationed at Camp Wasco in California's Central Valley. He wrote to his parents that he had just completed another week of dust and heat and sweat and was learning to fly with instruments:

> *It is done dual, the student sits on the back seat and flies with a black hood shutting out the outside world, leaving nothing but the instruments to watch. All instincts fail, you do not even have the sensation of flying, you cannot recognize the difference between straight and level, steep banks: even inverted flight; you can't tell when you are on your back even. The only thing to do is watch the instruments like a hawk, they will tell you what your position is in regard to the earth. It is a different kind of flying and hard to get accustomed to.*

A novice flyer, Ted describes "nose-overs" caused by dust filling the brakes, which were, he wrote, *"touchy as an old maid with a wig. If any weight is put on them, over they go, costing the government about $2,000. You have to use the brakes as though walking on a crate of eggs."* He thanks his mother for the candy, but advises her not to send any more because *"the ants eat it, the sun melts it, and it's so warm I don't feel the need for sweets."*

JOACHIM

On September 19, with fifty-seven victories to his credit, Joachim was promoted to Hauptmann (Captain) and assumed command of II Gruppe JG 26. The next two months were relatively quiet months for Joachim, but in November, he was asked to be a member of the honor guard at a Nazi State Funeral for Werner Mölders, the first flier in WWII to break the record set by the "Red Baron" (Manfred von Richthofen) in the First World War. In his memoir, Joachim's father, Paul Müncheberg, recalled the event commemorating Mölders' death:

I went on leave to Friedrichshof. One day Achim called from Knal, he had to quickly go to Berlin to stand in the honor guard with five other bearers of the Knight's Cross for Mölders who had fatally fallen in Breslau. He needed a new uniform for this, which was in the closet in Friedrichshof. Erika and I travelled that same day to Berlin and so we saw one another again after a long time. Erika and I received a personal invitation from Göring to attend Mölders' state funeral. It was especially formal, at the ministry and at the Louisen cemetery.

Ted

In the fall of 1941, Ted was in the next phase of his training, stationed at Luke Field in Arizona, where the schedule was intense:

We are going to ground school five days a week, but we are flying every day, seven days a week, which of course means not sleeping past 5:30 in the morning for a month. The ships we are flying, advanced trainers, are beautiful ships. They are heavier and faster than anything we have previously flown. The ship is a honey, but you have to watch her, like most lovely creatures, she can't be trusted when not being watched.

In November, about the same time Joachim was counting his 58th and 59th kills near Dunkirk, Ted wrote to his brother about his "Seven Minute Error."

Ordinarily seven minutes does not make much difference one way or another. A date will usually wait that length of time with no particular agrievement, but at 160 miles an hour cruising it does make a bit of a difference. Our instructors gave us about five minutes to chart a T and D (Time and Distance) problem, we were to intercept him at a given time over a little village known as Red Rock, and he would wait for us, thirty seconds one way or another. We had to borrow make-shift compasses and rulers to figure our course and with no time for a counter-check we had to be off. I was first to leave. I got to my first point with no difficulty and on schedule and proceeded to Red Rock. As it happened I had figured my time seven minutes too long on this hundred mile run, so when I got where I should be my watch said it was about twenty-five miles farther on when I was over the town. My heading and my seven minutes brought me well into the mountains. I circled the town it MIGHT have been for a bit, then after a few minutes I realized I was off course (but unaware of my error). I had not time to figure the bearing from the field to where I was, my chart had blown out of the canopy and there I was. I didn't have the right frequency coil to pick up the Phoenix beam, so I did the next best thing, head in the direction I THOUGHT was Phoenix and the field over strange country with no check points, towns or any recognizable places. The ceiling was 7,000 and below and the mountains 6,000 and above so I couldn't get any altitude to have a look around, just fly with the compass and dodge the higher mountains.

This went on for a considerable time, over one ridge, I would try to pick a forced-landing field, over others I would realize it would be necessary to jump in case of necessity. The country was barren, dry, completely cut up with gorges and ridges. Eventually my right tank was empty and I was on the twenty-gallon reserve in the left. I had picked up a road and was following it, the country was flatter, with a fair chance of a safe wheels-up landing. I noticed a small town, but didn't recognize it and a tiny civilian emergency field by it (used by Cubs, Porterfields, etc.) but I still thought I was headed right and the field was just over the next ridge so I went past it but checked my gas—three gallons, less than five minutes at most, so I returned to the "field" and dragged it, there was about a fifteen mile cross wind so I pulled up, came around again, dropped the wheels and flaps and managed to set it down short without a bounce. When I stopped rolling the town was out, all twenty-five people. They informed me that I was in Salome. I sent a wire (no telephone) and stood guard over the ship that night almost froze them off. [sic] The townsfolk were very nice though, bringing food, coffee, cigarettes. I couldn't leave the ship, of course. The next day an officer found the field (it isn't on any charts), I gassed up and we "buzzed" the town in formation, giving the good burgers a thrill.

When I got back to the barracks the boys had a reception planned, toilet paper led a path from the door to my bunk which was decorated with more of the same material in the form of a canopy and such appropriate cards as Welcome! The prodigal son returns to the fold!"

While Joachim's record brought him honors and to the attention of the Luftwaffe high command, Ted's failure to navigate a time and distance problem added a little comic relief to his friends in flight training. Perhaps no two images could be more illustrative of the vast gulf of experience that separated these two young men in the fall of 1941.

———

On December 7, 1941, at 7:55 a.m. Hawaii time, Japanese fighters began what would become a two-hour attack of Pearl Harbor, where two thousand four hundred servicemen lost their lives, twenty American ships, and more than three hundred airplanes were damaged or destroyed.

On December 8, the United States declared war on Japan, with only one dissenting voice: Jeanette Rankin, Republican from Montana and the first woman to have been elected to Congress in 1917.

———

Hitler had long predicted that Germany would fight the United States so when the third prong of the Axis triumvirate provoked the giant by attacking Pearl Harbor, he was delighted, "Now it is impossible for us to lose the war, we now have an ally who has never been vanquished in three thousand years." For his part, Joseph Goebbels, minster of propaganda noted, "The Führer is extremely pleased at this development...Now this is a world war in the truest sense of the word." [58]

In the following days, Japan attacked Thailand, Malaysia, and the Philippines, and sank the British Warships *Prince of Wales* and *Repulse* off the Malaysian coast. On December 11, in solidarity with its Asian partner, Germany declared war on the United States. A few hours later, the seventy-seventh Congress "authorized and directed the President to employ the entire naval and military forces of the United States and the resources of the Government to carry on war against the Government of Germany; and, to bring the conflict to a successful termination, all of the resources of the country are hereby pledged by the Congress of the United States."

On December 12, 1941, Second Lieutenant Theodore R. Sweetland wore his brand new, freshly starched uniform in the graduation ceremony at Luke Air Force Base in Arizona. In his diary Ted wrote: *Mother, Dad, Ruth and Carla all had a bit of a cry when talk was made of us fighting this nasty old war—possibilities had become actual.*

Ted's parents, his sister Ruth, and his girlfriend, Carla, could not know the future; they could only hope that Ted would be one of the lucky ones. They could pray, as his mother surely did, extracting a promise that he would wear the medal that had been blessed by Pope Pius XI three summers ago. Now the possibility of war had become a certainty for young Americans in the Armed Services and the family and friends at the ceremony knew that not everyone's loved one would return. By the time America entered the war, Germany had already lost 350,000 young men. Their average age was twenty-three, just two years older than Ted was that proud December day when he pinned his silver wings to his lapel.

On the day Ted graduated from the Air Force Academy, the pilot who would eventually kill him scored his sixty-second victory: A Royal Air Force Spitfire on the coast of France. Joachim then flew to Abbeville where his father, recently deployed to France after months on the Eastern Front, joined him to celebrate Christmas and the waning days of 1941.

*Ted on graduation day at Luke Air Force Base in
Arizona, December 12, 1941.*

*On the day Ted earned his wings, Joachim scored his sixtieth victory. Two weeks later,
Paul joined his son in France, near Abbeville, where they celebrated Christmas, 1941.*

CHAPTER 13

The Balance Begins to Tip

———

ON JANUARY 1, 1942, REPRESENTATIVES from twenty-six nations met in Washington D.C. to sign "The Atlantic Charter," a declaration of unity against the Axis dictatorships of Germany, Italy, and Japan. Each of the signatories to the document, which had been originally hammered out the previous August by Churchill and Roosevelt, pledged to employ their full resources, military or economic, against members of the Tripartite Pact and each government pledged not to make a separate armistice or peace with the enemies. There could be no clearer signal that Hitler had ignited a world war.

TED

Five days after the signing of the Atlantic Charter, Ted who was stationed at Hamilton AFB on the San Francisco Bay, tuned his radio to President Roosevelt's State of the Union address:

> *I am proud to say to you that the spirit of the American people was never higher than it is today—the Union was never more closely knit together—this country was never more deeply determined to face the solemn tasks before it.*
>
> *The response of the American people has been instantaneous, and it will be sustained until our security is assured....*
>
> *... But the dreams of empire of the Japanese and Fascist leaders were modest in comparison with the gargantuan aspirations of Hitler and his Nazis. Even before they came to power in 1933, their plans for that*

conquest had been drawn. Those plans provided for ultimate domina-
tion, not of any one section of the world, but of the whole earth and all
the oceans on it.

Ted was inspired by his president. As he imagined goose-stepping Nazis on the Champs Élysées or children in London running for shelter with bombers screaming overhead, he was proud to wear the uniform he had worked hard to earn.

At Hamilton, Ted was assigned to what he called the "best outfit in the world", the 77th Pursuit Squadron in the 20th Group, but even before they left San Francisco in January, two of his squadron mates lost control of their planes and spun in, driving the plane and themselves into the unyielding ground. Two more of his classmates died in bad weather, cause unknown. From the beginning until the end of the war, America lost an average of 170 planes each day, many from accidents or inexperience; over the course of the war, 40,000 American pilots died in combat.[59]

JOACHIM

During the early part of 1942, Joachim was where he wanted to be: on the Western Front racking up victories over France, Britain and the Channel. In January, he got a call from his best friend and brother-in-law, Heinz: He and Eva had had a son, and they wanted "Uncle Achim" to be his godfather.

Konrad Helmut Joachim Hoffstätter was christened a few months later just as spring was beginning to dress the countryside. The family gathered in the great room downstairs near the fireplace in the same two-story home where Joachim had been born on a cold winter morning twenty-three years earlier. In the back of the house, birch and aspen leaves were beginning to shimmer and the earth where the snow had receded was a mosaic of green against the rich black soil. The promise of new life was everywhere, including in Joachim's arms, where towheaded Konrad peered with wide blue eyes at his godfather who had flown from France to celebrate a birth in a world where death was everywhere.

TED

In January 1942, the 77th Pursuit Squadron made the cross-country trip to North Carolina. Ted's flight was uneventful, but he was met on the East Coast with news of a close friend's death:

When we got to Wilmington N.C. I found some bad news—Werner Von Berkefelt had been killed—down straight into the ocean from 8000 feet. No apparent explanation (He might have been unconscious.) We had gone through flying school together all the way, from primary on. He used to tell me that if he ever washed-out of flying school he would join the RAF immediately (before we entered the war). Flying meant more than anything else in the world—I believe even more than life itself. When we were rained in at Myrtle Beach we used to sit in our tents by a fire and shoot the breeze and play poker. "Where's Von?" He was out sitting in a P-40 just looking at the instruments and feeling the controls...all that was ever found of him was a piece of lung and a piece of rib the size of your little finger. Shook accompanied the remains home in a sealed casket. Shook and he were great friends. It's a dirty job.

For Ted, Werner was not a statistic, he was a person with whom he had worked and played, a friend whose parentage was clearly German, though Ted did not note that fact in his diary and he likely didn't even note it in his head. That the guys shortened Werner's name to the preposition "von", meaning "from" which signals aristocracy is pretty classically American. Ted's own last name, shortened to "Sweetie" by his mates, was once a farm in Scotland, but Ted didn't think of himself as Scottish any more than he would have thought of his friend Von as German. For Ted, they were simply part of the American patchwork where of the 123 million citizens counted in 1930, fifty-three million were either foreign-born or children of foreign-born parents. Looking European helped and not everyone felt welcome. German-Americans were certainly shunned during the war by many who blamed Germany for the hell their sons were living—and dying in. Japanese-Americans could not hide their ancestry and after Pearl Harbor many were forced to move to Relocation

Camps east of the Sierra Nevada. There were no men with Japanese surnames in Ted's squadron, though there were many Japanese-Americans who served America fully, honorably, and many times to their death.

On March 3, 1942, Ted wrote a letter to his brother, Jack:

I think God has a special little room off in a corner of heaven that's filled with smoke and good whiskey where all the guys that wouldn't stay on the ground go. All they do is smoke and drink and tell about the time -----

"There I was flat on my back at 200 feet. The engine konked. What did I do? I spun in."

"Were you hurt?"

"I'm here ain't I?"

The conversation will center exclusively on these subjects: flying, women, and flying.

In June, to Ted's dismay, he continued to be stationed at Hotel Cape Fear in North Carolina, and wrote to his parents to tell them: *I am an instructor and don't like it at all and am doing everything I can to get a boat trip.*

He didn't get a boat trip immediately, but he did get transferred to Myrtle Beach, where more of his buddies were stationed. Accidents were not unusual and had become somewhat of a spectator sport for the locals.

We had fun at Myrtle, buzzing (low fly up) the field and beach. Riley and I chased a cop off his motorcycle on the beach and into the sand. There was a 90 degree curved ditch at the field in front of the operations tent and we would see who could put his wing in deepest at 200+ mph. It was good sport.

This time of the year we were killing off better than one pilot a week, crowds used to come to the field on Sunday afternoons to see the accidents and were seldom disappointed. One boy hit near where I was sleeping and he and the ship bounded completely over the ten-foot wire and barb fence before disintegrating, not touching a strand of the wire.

Three of the fellows had accidents which completely ruined their nerve for pursuit thereby probably saving their lives. For what?

One boy, Pierce, cut down three trees broke the fuselage in half, clipped off both wings and sent the engine ten feet ahead of the ship, jumped his canopy strut and sat in the ship waiting for fire. They chopped him out with axes. He suffered a minor scalp injury. Three months later he was killed in Alaska, forced down in to the ocean in a P-39 with a belly-tank. Never came to the surface.

Old Keith Fedde spun into the ocean a mile from where his wife was staying. She waited four days for the remains. They found the ship and a small piece of his helmet, but no Fedde. Perhaps God wanted him intact. At any rate she went home, alone. A few days later she sent the Squadron Commander, Jason, a bouquet of flowers with the request he drop them where her husband went down…It is better, though harder, to love and suffer than not feel the powerful emotions so closely allied. May God's grace be with you, oh lonely heart!

Keith was an honest good natured man. We missed him.

Ted and his mother before his deployment, both have pilot's wings pinned to their lapels.

Death had become matter-of-fact, and Ted wasn't even in combat yet. The scene he describes sounds like a picnic with spectators gathering for an afternoon of entertainment. He seems to report friends' deaths more dispassionately than he notes the survival of those who have lost their nerve as did three of his colleagues who survived crashes and lived. But for what, he asks? He is not immune to the tragedy that death brings to loved ones, like Keith's wife, but he does not seem to fear his own death so much as he repeatedly laments not being in the middle of the action, which he craves. It's consistent with his personality that he satisfies his need for adventure and adrenaline by taking unnecessary risks, like dipping a wing into a ditch.

JOACHIM

In June, while Ted was buzzing the locals at Myrtle Beach, the *Wehrmacht Communique* noted that Joachim had downed two Spitfires near Abbeville within six minutes, bringing his score to eighty victories. On June 5, he was awarded the German cross in Gold and ten days later, the coveted Swords were added to his Knight's Cross.

The new medals were a welcome addition to his uniform and just in time to wear as he traveled to Berlin to compete in the Light Athletics Championships. He and his brother-in-law, Heinz, had long dreamed of competing in the Olympic Games, which would not resume until 1948, long after it was too late for both young men. They were not Olympic games, but the sport championships at the arena where he had witnessed the Olympic athletes compete in 1936, provided a welcome break from the front. Joachim did well, adding to his notoriety in Germany as both an accomplished pilot and competitive athlete.

After an interval of several weeks, Joachim was sent to the Eastern Front with JG 51 where his first victories were just five minutes apart. One biographer suggested this feat may have inspired over-confidence as he was subsequently shot down twice in quick succession, but he was not badly injured and two days later, after the Commodore of JG 51 was put out of action, Joachim took command of the squadron.

*In the summer of 1942, Joachim took a break from the front to
compete in decathlon events in the Light Athletics
Championship in Berlin.*

Several pages of his album are devoted to the publicity shots his fame gen-
erated, but there is one picture that was never made public. It was taken at the
Wolf's Lair, Hitler's headquarters in East Prussia. The framing of the picture
is a perfect triangle: two young men on the right, facing Adolf Hitler on the
left. The name of the young man behind is not known, but the young man

in front is clearly Joachim. He is standing straight, with his gold-braided hat in his left hand, against his side. His right arm is outstretched and his elbow straight. Joachim is slightly taller than Hitler whose hand is reaching towards him. In the middle of the dark portrait the two arms extended towards each other form a V, and at the very center, Joachim's young hand is clasped in Hitler's grasp.

The portrait, taken by Heinrich Hoffmann, Hitler's personal photographer, is powerful, more powerful than medals or postcards. At the Wolf's Lair, Joachim was photographed in the very center of the vortex of evil in a sacred ceremony of recognition. Joachim wore the Knight's Cross with Oak Leaves and Swords, signaling his role, a particular and well-defined one that was part of a much larger plan. A knight of the air, Joachim was much closer to the center of power than most of the young men who were fighting and dying for the man to whom they had sworn allegiance and whose hand Joachim had taken in his own.

Hitler was known for extended handshakes; in a photograph, a handshake lasts forever. The Führer is leaning slightly forward, his knuckles look clenched around Joachim's hand, his lips are pursed in a kind of smile and his gaze is steady, like a snake.

The hand that Joachim extended to the Führer was the same one he used to pressure the trigger in his Messerschmitt to shoot down planes and their pilots who would twirl to their deaths as they spun to earth. These enemy dead were not part of the ceremony of recognition, commemorated in the cavernous interior of the Wolf's Lair. Nor is there room for a mother in this dark picture, or a little blond godson. There is only the war hero and the man to whom he had sworn allegiance and for whom he had been long prepared to give his life. The path to this moment of glory had begun long ago, when Hitler's tinny voice exhorted fourteen-year-old Joachim and all the youth at the Nuremburg Rally to give their lives so that the Third Reich would live on. *We will die but Germany will live on in you. When there is nothing of us then you must hold in your fists the flags that we hoisted out of nothing....* Joachim had a duty to do, as did every member of the Volksgemeinschaft. He did his job well and he was rewarded.

Joachim with Adolf Hitler at the Wolf's Lair, Hitler's headquarters on the Eastern Front. In September 1942, Joachim became the thirteenth fighter pilot to receive the Knight's Cross with Swords.

TED

In September 1942, Ted was in Fort Dix, New Jersey when he received orders: He would be boarding a ship bound for Britain. His letter to his parents after he heard the news begins with small talk, but it quickly turns into a farewell.

> *Under existing circumstances, I find it almost necessary to wax philosophical—of thought how you, Mother & Dad, have given me so many advantages, of your sacrifices to do what you knew was right for not only me but all us children, of small thanks for all your troubles. This, to me, is*

what makes a person, a people, or a nation great, countless sacrifices great and small through a lifetime—selfless striving to make our world a little easier for the other man. It is not flash-in-the-pan heroism but a strongly burning courage that lightens the shadows of doubt and despair. After all that is fundamentally all we are fighting for — the right to help ourselves and those we love to live a God-like life; and it will only be with <u>His</u> help that we will succeed.

In a subsequent letter, written shortly before he sailed, Ted wrote:

Do not expect to hear from me for a while, but know that you are always in my thoughts. If an unusually long period of time goes by without you hearing from me, do not worry because communication is difficult now and will be worse later. If anything did happen to me the War Department would notify you immediately, so no news is good news. …Night bombings are very interesting to watch…Don't worry about not hearing from me…

On September 16, 1942, Ted wrote his first letter from Britain, noting that the trans-Atlantic crossing was without event. The short note ends with a request: *Mom if you happen to knit a few extra dark red socks about Dad's size I know two feet that would be glad to wear them.*

JOACHIM

In September 1942, Joachim was on the Eastern Front fighting what the Germans called "The Crusade Against Bolshevism" and what the Russians, fighting in their homeland, called "The Patriotic War." The Third Reich's conquest of the massive Soviet Territory was supposed to have been quick, but the front was long, and the supply of Russian men and women seemed inexhaustible. Both Hitler and Stalin were ruthless leaders and the punishment for desertion was death. In July 1942, Stalin issued "Order No. 227" also known as "Not One Step Backward" that authorized blocking brigades to shoot any Russian soldier who tried to flee. Hitler echoed this command, refusing to allow General Paulus to evacuate Stalingrad, setting the stage for the annihilation of the German Sixth Army by a lethal combination of enemy fire, winter, and starvation.

During August and September, 1942, Joachim flew scores of missions on the Eastern Front. His first three kills were recorded on August 8, five minutes apart. His hundredth victory was over Kubinka, seventy kilometers southwest of Moscow: An American built P-39 air cobra, evidence that America's Lend-Lease program was supporting the Russian efforts against the invading army.

On September 27, 1942, Joachim scored his 116th and last victory in the East. With thirty-two bars added to the tail of his red-hearted Messerschmitt, he was named "Commodore" of the 77th and sent south and across the Mediterranean to North Africa.

TED

By the end of September 1942, Ted was in England, getting closer, but still some distance from the action. His duties were largely administrative as he was assigned to solving a host of logistical challenges, but he was also flying Spitfires. To his diary Ted confides that the most fun he had in England was flying to the Midlands to see his old classmates.

> *We sat around at the club and drank and talked till the wee hours. How good it is to see fellows with whom you have shared the same difficulties again. I think there were as glad to see me as I they.*
>
> *"How's Tuck?"*
>
> *"Oh, he's off on an island drinking coconut milk and thinking of 'Frisco."*
>
> *"Dam I'd like to see him again. What happened to old Virgil?"*
>
> *"He was on the same island. Went out on a patrol mission and just never came back.*
>
> *"No. That's tough. He was a good old boy."*
>
> *"Yea. Oh, what about Pennington?"*

"He came across with the 1ˢᵗ and got the Flying Medal but it was posthumous. Went into the Atlantic somewhere. They sent a Hudson out to look for him but all they could find was a sub, which they sank.

Damany I'd like to join those boys. As you may or may not deduce, I do not like sitting around a command one wit.

JOACHIM

One of Joachim's first actions as commander of the 77ᵗʰ squadron in North Africa was to adopt the red heart, long emblazoned on his fuselage as his squadron emblem. From October of 1942 on, the 77th was known as the "Red Hearts." His men liked Joachim, who was nearly always quiet in the cockpit. On base, though, he would sometimes take out his accordion, bringing some German music to the dusty desert. His long-haired dachshund, Seppl, was everyone's friend and the squadron's mascot.

To his frustration, his promotion to Commander meant that he was spending less time in the cockpit and more time doing paperwork and managing logistics, which was not what he liked to do. Like Ted, Joachim sought action. He wanted to be in the air.

He was perhaps right. Germany's hold on North Africa was weakening as Rommel's beleaguered army faced the overwhelming power of Bernard Montgomery's forces, known as the "British" Eighth, though the troops came from throughout the Commonwealth and also included exiles from Nazi-occupied territories. Out-numbered nearly two to one both on the ground and in the air, the Germans were struggling in the Battle of El Alamein, which had begun on October 23, and ended ten days later with victory for the Allies. The situation in Egypt was growing dire for Germany and in a rare moment of insubordination, Rommel acted against Hitler's express orders, and retreated along with his decimated Afrika Korps to Libya.

The end of the Battle of El Alamein coincided almost precisely with the beginning of the Allied invasion of North Africa, dubbed Operation Torch. As 75,000 Allied troops landed on the continent from Casablanca to Algiers, the challenges for Joachim and every commander under Axis leadership multiplied. Neither Hitler nor Mussolini had anticipated that the invasion of Europe would be through the soft underbelly of North Africa and, fortuitously for the Allies the Axis lines were already stretched thin as they struggled in Stalingrad and the Caucasus.

TED

As Joachim's squadron gathered in Libya, Ted was traveling by train from England to Scotland to board the converted British liner, the *Dunnotter Castle* and head out to sea. He and five other officers threw their duffels in bunks bolted in layers to the bulkheads in a cabin that had been originally designed for two. They did not know where they were headed, but there were bets going—Libya, Egypt, around the Cape of Good Hope. It wasn't until they were underway that they learned they were bound for North Africa. They were told their landing would be somewhere in Morocco, Algeria, or Tunisia. Many of the men aboard the ship could not have placed any of these countries on a map.

On board the *Dunnotter Castle*, the men drilled, took deck watch, prepared for mess and bunk inspections, and enjoyed three meals a day supplemented by morning and afternoon tea. His troop ship rendezvoused with what Ted described as a vast convoy. The weather was generally fair, and Ted had a lot of time to read, finishing Thackeray's *Vanity Fair* and Tolstoy's *War and Peace*, sitting in the sea-fresh air on the sunny side of the deck.

The Dunnotter Castle was one of over five hundred ships, carrying seventy-thousand men who were all part of Operation Torch, the coordinated Allied invasion of North Africa. Hundreds of ships from Britain joined over a hundred sailing from America. Traveling eastward into the Mediterranean, they passed Tangiers, lit up like a Christmas tree, but the Rock of Gibraltar was black and nearly swallowed by the night. How very different yet how very much the same it was as the first time he had seen the Rock that summer of 1938, growing bulkier on the horizon as he had stood at the rail with Gloria by his side. They had been dancing and the cool evening air felt fresh and welcome. He remembered the way the light of the full moon shimmered on the sea and ignited the bow wave.

On November 8, 1942, there was no moon and the lights that had adorned the Rock in 1938, were all doused. Only the heavens were alight, flickering and infinite, like the sea that surrounded them, dark and deep and hiding U-boats on the hunt. Beneath the black monolithic promontory of the Rock of Gibraltar, in what was described as his "badly ventilated office six hundred feet underground"[60] General Dwight D. Eisenhower, the commander of the Allied Forces, was working long hours as the men he had called into action steamed by.

Even as the convoys left the British Isles and America, no one knew what to expect from the French. After just seven weeks of fighting, France had capitulated to Hitler's forces in June of 1940. The resulting armistice divided the country into two zones. The north of France was occupied and completely under Germany's control; the southern portion and French colonies in Africa were under the control of a government that had been constituted at Vichy and was headed up by Marshall Philippe Pétain, who was French, but swore allegiance to Hitler.

The operation had been planned without knowing what, exactly, the French under the Vichy government would do. Would they be loyal to their country that was now occupied by Nazis or would they be loyal to the puppet government the Nazis had put in place?

By the time the troops were sailing towards the coast, Allied informants knew the answer: the French would be loyal to Hitler. Unfortunately, the Allies never received a coded alert sent to Gibraltar from a radio transmitter in Oran, "Expect resistance everywhere." When the first wave landed at Oran where Ted's troop ship was headed, nine thousand Vichy French defenders attacked the Allies who had left their ports in Britain and America believing that Europe was united in their fight against the Nazis.

The roar of the battle drowned out the loudspeakers through which Allies speaking American-accented French attempted to persuade the defending French forces that they were coming in peace; they would liberate France and their territories! The Vichy French troops did not yield and though the battle was not long, it was a baptism by fire for the Americans. Nearly 500 Allies were killed and over 700 were wounded; French losses were three times that, but after a day and a half, at noon on November 10, Oran fell and the big blue pennant, signaling Allied success, was raised over the city.

The *Dunnotter Castle* was part of a slower convoy, scheduled to arrive after the port was secure and they were still approaching when they learned that

Oran had fallen, but not without a fight. Ted and the other men on board were tense. Their ship had already dodged several torpedoes and they knew they had been spotted by an unidentified enemy plane. As the rippling coast of Algiers loomed on the near horizon, Ted watched as a freighter hit by an unseen torpedo tipped, wallowed, and sank below the inky surface of the water. Finally, as dusk fell over the now subdued city, the *Dunnotter Castle* docked. Ted's diary notes are terse:

Arrived in North Africa. We spent 24 hours dodging one sub pack and another let us have 4 torpedoes, all of which went wild. The Corvettes let loose ash cans; those depth charges make a lot of noise. Tied up without further incident and marched 12 miles with packs. It was a pretty rugged drag as we were out of shape. Blisters didn't make it easier. Arrived eventually at the airport of Oran, which is a bit beat up from American fire and French sabotage...Had to sleep on the springs in my coat as our bedding rolls had not arrived... Shaving facilities are a bit primitive—we shave in our steel helmets with cold water. The airport is very colorful literally – pink buildings, etc. A lot of damaged aircraft on the field.

Over the next few weeks, Ted spent eighteen hours traveling ninety-five miles by train from La Sénia to Orleansville, which was closer to Italy's colony, Libya, where the Axis controlled the ports and landing fields. Trains were so slow, the men sometimes got out to walk alongside the cars that were loaded like an ark with chickens, turkeys, and screaming pigs. In town, they were accosted by children pestering them for chewing gum and cigarettes. If no treats were forthcoming Ted wrote, *one of the men would yell at the urchins and then they really showed their knowledge of backstreet English with a list of curse words that surprises even us.* In Biskra, the oldest oasis on the Sahara, Ted was reunited with some of the buddies he had trained with, though he was well aware that since they had last seen each other, much had changed. They had seen combat and he had not.

Finally, here I found the outfit, renewed acquaintance with MacDonald, Pope, and Aitken[61] and met new fellows, fine chaps they are too. It was a bit ticklish, joining a new outfit that has just returned from combat with a good record, me a stranger to most and with more rank than my classmates—being in the background for a week or so until they decided to accept me as one of them. I am very glad that I got along with them as they are damn good men.

JOACHIM

As the Allies continued to land in Morocco and Algeria, Joachim, who had been promoted to Major just a month earlier, faced his men in Bir-el-Arca. He could not know that it would take Oran just one day to fall, though he probably found out at about the same time Hitler did that the Allies had also made nine landings along the Barbary Coast, from Casablanca to Algiers and several points in between.

The Afrika Korps had pushed well into Egypt, but though his position on the coast less than fifty miles from the Suez Canal was unsustainable, Rommel's unauthorized retreat after the Battle of El Alamein provoked ire from the leadership in Germany, whose philosophy was to stand firm, regardless of the cost in human lives. Hermann Göring, commander-in-chief of the Luftwaffe, wrote a letter that he ordered be read by all the commanders in Africa to all their men. In the letter, Göring blames the Luftwaffe for Rommel's failure. If the pilots, Göring wrote, had been doing their job, Rommel would not have failed at El Alamein.[62]

Like the rest of the Luftwaffe, the 77th squadron had also pulled back to safe territory inside Libya. The men facing their commander knew that Göring's accusation was untrue and Joachim knew it, too. For him, the missive underscored how out of touch the command in Germany was with the reality in the field. The pilots were being blamed for conditions over which they had no control: distances were great, supplies couldn't get past the increased Allied presence in the Mediterranean; they were outnumbered; Hitler had over-reached and the men Joachim addressed that day were among those who were paying the price. Joachim did as he was told. He read the letter aloud. But he added a postscript. He told his men, "We will not leave this place."

The men of Jagdeschwader 77 would neither retreat nor surrender. One of the pilots under Joachim's command confided his frustration to his diary:

*As we are receiving no supplies, when we have no aircraft left we are sup-
posed to pick up a rifle and fight to the end with the Africa Corps, and if
necessary go down with it. Müncheberg said that we will probably never
see Europe again."[63]*

As Oran fell, Hitler ordered German and Italian troops to occupy Vichy France
and he gave Field Marshal Albert Kesselring (who had orchestrated the terror
bombings of Warsaw, Coventry, and the campaign against Russia) absolute
authority over all ground and air forces in the Mediterranean. On November
24, Kesselring flew to Libya to meet with his commanders. Joachim was in
the group, gathered at the Italian Marble Arch on the border of the ancient
cities of Carthage and Cyrene. The massive travertine monument had been
unveiled in an extravagant night ceremony that Mussolini attended in 1937,
to commemorate the legend of two brothers from Carthage who chose to be
buried alive rather than yield territory to their enemies. In the next weeks and
months, a fraternity of men from countries around the globe and on both sides
of the war would give their lives so as not to yield ground across North Africa.

On Thanksgiving Day 1942, a terrible battle previewed the desperate see-
sawing to come in North Africa. Staccato shots seemingly from nowhere and
everywhere peppered the ground and ricocheted off tanks. Young Americans
who had approached the idea of battle with audacious courage died in the
mud clutching their rifles, some burned beyond recognition were entombed
in their tanks. Rain-muddy rivulets ran crimson. The German-American
tank battle ended with enormous casualties on both sides, but when the battle
was over, the Allies had gained brief and tenuous control over Medjez-el-Bab,
the key to the backdoor of Tunisia. The scene, with temporary victors on both
sides, would be repeated again and again. It was a war of attrition that the
Axis powers did not have the resources to win.

TED

Eisenhower had moved his headquarters from the Rock of Gibraltar closer
to the front and was enjoying his Thanksgiving dinner of roasted peacock,
cabbage and peas, served with Algerian rosé [64] in Algiers. Ted's Thanksgiving

fare did not compare favorably: cold mutton stew, hardtack, and ersatz coffee brewed from pulverized dates, the color and taste of ink. But Ted was grateful to be where he was: deployed, finally, in North Africa, assigned to the 52nd Fighter Group, attached to the 4th *so I can knock a little rust off before going to work against ME 109's and FW 190's.*[65] *Thank God I can now do what I want or at any rate hope for the opportunity of doing what I want.*

What he wanted was combat, and that would come, but while the Allies had landed en masse along the Barbary Coast from Morocco to Algiers in early November, the Allied command structure was problematic. Relationships remained fractious, split by rivalries between the British and American leaders, feelings that trickled down to the men who wondered if any of their commanders knew what they were doing. For both British and Americans, their new French allies tangled the web of loyalty even farther. After their surrender, the French soldiers were allowed to keep only the most antiquated equipment. Their allegiance, as the Allies had learned at Oran, was uncertain.

Men died because reconnaissance was sketchy and logistics were a nightmare. The only American tanks that rumbled east for the first battles in North Africa were death traps armed with a "squirrel rifle" – a 37 mm gun whose shells pinged harmlessly off the heavy German tanks. It was only later that they would discover that the ammunition the men were using was designed for training and was not combat grade.

With seven airfields and twenty squadrons of nine planes each in Tunisia, the Luftwaffe had massive air superiority over the Allies whose closest airfield was at Bone, fifty miles from the Tunisian border. Before Ted joined them, his squadron, the fifty-second, had flown from Bone for thirty-seven days, but had, by their own admission, little impact. They only had eight usable aircraft and when they flew sweeps deep into enemy territory German fighters swarmed them, often outnumbering their cluster of Spitfires three to one. Years later, the Pulitzer prize winning author, Rick Atkinson, summarized the situation this way, "By late November, only half the Allied planes in North Africa were still airworthy; American pilots also lost nearly twice as many aircraft to crashes and other mishaps than to combat, a ratio described by one commander as 'rather appalling.' The Allied air command was disorganized, poorly coordinated, and split by rivalry and national chauvinism."[66]

None of this confusion was aired in the media, since "Draconian censorship was imposed, with correspondents advised that no dispatches would be allowed that made people at home feel unhappy."[67] Nor did the men at the front know what was happening beyond what was immediately in front of them. Ernie Pyle, whose syndicated columns were published in over two hundred newspapers nationwide in the 1940s, wrote sensitive, poetic portraits of real men fighting a real war, but he was never critical and he never paints a picture of the carnage that he witnessed on the ground as he traveled with the infantry from Oran to Tunisia.

The challenges of men in the air were very different from those of the ground troops, who sweltered as they marched under the midday sun, or baked inside metal tanks so hot you could fry an egg on the gun turret. Dysentery, parasites, and trench foot were not uncommon, but Ted flying above them could not imagine the war from their point of view and failed to imagine how startling troops on the move might not be amusing to men who had been on the march, or seen combat.

The other day I was flying low over bivouacked troops – it's fun to see their startled expression when they suddenly see an airplane, possibly an enemy. I tried to fly so low they couldn't hit me but had to pull up over a hill and one of the boys hit me in the elevator with what looked like a .50 cal. He almost missed—a good shot. It was patched easily.

Ted was so young, as were most of those who fought. He sought what the recruiting brochures promised: the high drama of action and adventure. As Ernie Pyle wrote,

In the magazine the war seemed romantic and exciting, full of heroics and vitality...Was war dramatic or not? Certainly there were great tragedies, unbelievable heroism, even a constant undertone of comedy. But when I sat down to write, I saw instead: men at the front suffering and wishing they were somewhere else, men in routine jobs just behind the lines bellyaching because they couldn't get to the front, all of them desperately hungry for somebody to talk to besides themselves, no women to be heroes in front of, damned little wine to drink, precious little song, cold and fairly dirty, just toiling from day to day in a world full of insecurity, discomfort, homesickness, and a dulled sense of danger.[68]

War had given Ted purpose; the Air Force had given him a team. Flying low over bivouacked troops was a thoughtless prank, but after months of waiting for action, he might be forgiven for such an explosion of exuberance. In the air he could forget the great hollow emptiness that plagued him at his administrative job and inevitably accompany those times in life that are without either the exaltation of the highs or the desperation of the lows. In that passive void where there is neither excitement nor meaning, there is, simply, existence; a quietude that those who have seen combat often seek in vain to find again.

JOACHIM

Italian and German troops were no longer battling only the nations of Europe; Allied forces in North Africa included Indian, South African, New Zealand, Australian and American troops all pushing east towards Tunis. Rommel's retreat was followed by another Allied victory as the day after Thanksgiving, British infantrymen captured the dusty, abandoned town of Tébourba. From the nearby hill, dubbed Point 186 for its height in meters, the Allies could see their objective, Tunis, its graceful minarets piercing the morning mist like slender stalagmites. Visible, too, were the German gull-winged precision bombers, Stukas, taking off from the airfield just a few kilometers away bearing their lethal loads. When a Stuka dives, it shrieks; it is a sound that terrorized servicemen and civilians across Europe.

As battles raged in the air and on the ground from Tunis, across Libya and into Egypt, the frontline was pushed east and west, north and south. In early December, the JG 77 "Red Hearts" assisted the German armored forces to break through Allied positions, forcing the Allies west again towards Algeria. In the little town of Tébourba, in Tunisia, near the coast, bodies of young men who had come to the desert to defeat the Nazis were stacked for evacuation. Wounded men deafened by the din stumbled west in exhausted retreat. Many never moved at all.

During the attacks, Joachim added several more stripes to his plane's well-plumed tail, but for the first time, his victims were not RAF pilots. During the first two weeks of December, Joachim shot down three P-40's, every one of them had a single, easily identifiable marking: a white star against a round blue background, the symbol of the United States Army Air Corps.

Ted

As he navigated the political messiness of Vichy France, Eisenhower chose to appoint the man who had acted as Hitler's puppet, French Admiral Darlan, to the position of civil and military chief in North Africa. The decision was controversial as Darlan's sympathies were with the fascists and his actions had aided the Nazis even as the Allies landed on North Africa to liberate France. In America, Edward R. Murrow, the popular broadcast journalist, wrote, "Are we fighting the Nazis or sleeping with them?"

Eisenhower did not trust Darlan; he knew well that he was a quisling and a political liability, but Churchill and Roosevelt endorsed his decision, thinking that Darlan could be an asset, a belief that proved unfounded. Darlan was an opportunist without a moral center; he imprisoned thousands who had helped the Allies land, kept anti-Semitic laws in place, hoarded supplies of sugar and coffee in his home, and employed hundreds of press censors to jam BBC broadcasts so that what was happening in North Africa could not be heard by North Africans. The British Foreign Office cabled the American Embassy in Washington, "We are fighting for international decency and Darlan is the antithesis of this."[69] Darlan's assassination by a French national on Christmas Eve 1942, was somewhat of a gift for the Allies, though the assassin himself was tried, convicted, and executed for committing murder.

The men on the ground were not privy to inside information and knew almost nothing of the political machinations that were plaguing their leaders. They didn't get much news and what they got was censored, but morale was relatively high and the logisticians had made sure that mail from home would make it to the front for Christmas. Ted received two letters and one package, the red socks he had asked his mother to knit for him. It was, he wrote, *the best present he had ever received—a concrete embodiment of love; every stitch a knot of devotion between mother and son.*

I can see you now Mom sitting in your green chair in the sitting room with maybe a fire going and perhaps Ellen Todd and or John boy or other members of the family coming and going. The conversations and the warmth, the kind of warmth that comes because it is home. …. That's only part of what those socks meant to me.

Ted had longed to be in battle and was glad to be with his buddies, moving ever closer to the front. He does not hint of homesickness in his letters, but the socks gave him pause as they represented home and family and all the warmth and happiness and love he had left behind. At some point, on the inside cover of his battered diary, Ted wrote: *Oh! Vanitas Vanitatum! Which of us is happy in this world? Which of us has his desire? Or having it, is satisfied?*

———

A year had passed since that long ago day when Pearl Harbor was bombed. A year during which Joachim flew hundreds of sorties over Britain, France, the Low Countries, Yugoslavia, Russia, Libya, Algeria and Tunisia. During those twelve months, he shot down sixty planes, to end the year with an impressive total of one hundred and twenty-two victories. During this time, Ted had learned to fly; he had taught young recruits how to fly; he had perfected an unexpected maneuver as he practiced turning his agile fighter against the spin of the prop; he had managed logistical nightmares in England and North Africa. He had familiarized himself with the Spitfire in England and over the Mediterranean, where he scanned the horizon for signs of the enemy. He jotted a few notes in his diary.

The water, after so much time looking out loses all sense of perspective. We spotted two life rafts at different times, both empty. At first they looked no larger than sardine tins and it takes time to realize they might contain people. The occupants had left, by one way or another.

Historians look back at 1942 as the year the tide turned against the Axis powers. Though there was an enormous price being paid, Russia was holding its ground in the East and Britain, at last, was no longer alone. There would be a learning curve as Allies from different countries, often speaking different languages, learned to fight together. There would be major failures in leadership as Eisenhower struggled to minimize the political reality of dealing with a French government that had so recently capitulated to Hitler, and as generals in the field learned the terrain and the tricks that Erwin Rommel, Germany's wily Desert Fox, had long employed. For Americans, the war had barely begun and they were fighting a well-seasoned machine, but the Allies had deep resources and the American Industrial Complex was ramped up and had more to give.

Joachim knew that the future of the Third Reich was not bright. His men were exhausted; the supply lines were stretched to the breaking point and all the experience in the world could not overcome an empty fuel tank. Early in 1943, he would travel to Germany for what would turn out to be his last home leave. While there, he sat across the table from Hermann Göring and, in solidarity with his commanding officer and the men he commanded in the field, he would commit treason.

Ted Sweetland in Thélepte, Tunisia.

Joachim Müncheberg in La Fauconnerie, Tunisia.

CHAPTER 14

In the Air Stars Cross

———

FOR EIGHT DAYS IN MID-JANUARY 1943, American President Franklin Roosevelt and British Prime Minister Winston Churchill met in Casablanca, Morocco to discuss and confirm Anglo-American war policy. Though not all the Americans around the table agreed, at Churchill's insistence, "Hitler's extinction" took priority over the defeat of Japan, and a cross-Channel invasion would not be initiated until North Africa was secure. Since the Operation Torch landings, the Allies had taken a beating. Territory had been won then lost; air defense was limp; relationships between generals were fraught. The Allies had calculated ammunition based on WWI use, and though there were now half as many men in each division, modern guns used twice as many shells and bullets.

Perhaps most distressing of all, Dwight D. Eisenhower, Commander of all of the Allied Forces landing in North Africa, was not proving to be an effective leader. By December, 180,000 American troops had arrived in North Africa, but many of the men couldn't move because not enough vehicles had been shipped. Eisenhower himself did not set foot in Tunisia until Christmas Eve 1942, when winter rains were already making a muddy slough of the terrain and supply trains could not keep pace with the numbers of battalions attempting to move eastward. North Africa was dominated by two German armies, one led by Erwin Rommel, the infamous Desert Fox, and the other by Hans-Jürgen von Arnim, who had served the Führer ably in Poland, France, and the Soviet Union. Dislodging these two formidable enemies would require time and strategy.

Eisenhower was familiar with the business of war. He had worked as an aide to General Pershing, commander of U.S. forces during World War I, and as an aide to General MacArthur, the Army's chief of staff. He graduated first in his class at the Command General Staff College in Kansas, but he had never been Number One and his background was proving to be a ball and chain.

As Eisenhower sorted through administrative details that should have been assigned to aides, he had little time left for strategic oversight of military operations. He was a three-star general, outranked by the British generals in the field, but Roosevelt was reluctant to promote him until he had proved his mettle. Ultimately Eisenhower would earn that fourth star and one more besides, but he was facing a steep learning curve. Forced in January by his commander in chief to commit to a date when Tunisia would fall, Eisenhower said by spring.

The Allies, he promised, would be able to declare victory in Africa by June, maybe as early as mid-May. At a cost of many thousands of lives, planes, tanks, and armored vehicles, this objective would be realized.

JOACHIM

As the year turned, the Red Hearts were engaged in fewer aerial battles and Joachim and some of his men were able to take a little time off to go gazelle hunting. As his biographer notes, "Whenever possible, Joachim used this quiet time to go hunting for gazelles with comrades from the staff or the squadron. He shared a passion for hunting with many other pilots, and not only numerous aircraft but also many wild animals were victims of his marksmanship."[70]

In the middle of the relative quiet, there was also a day that Joachim described as "hell." Fierce Sirocco winds whipped the desert sand into gritty storm clouds, obliterated vision and flayed exposed skin. Joachim's group's war diary recorded two hundred and forty Allied planes in the Bir Dufan area, on the coast, not far east of Tripoli. On January 14, as the Allies initiated their offensive with heavy bomb attacks on the German front lines, Joachim and his team took to the air. Four minutes apart, Joachim shot down two P-40's. The squadron total for the day was twenty-eight aerial victories to the Allies nineteen. They had won the day, but it would not be enough.

With a total of 129 confirmed scores, Joachim flew home to the Fatherland for a scheduled break. He spent time skiing in Austria and visiting Friedrichshof where his mother and sister were managing the business of the estate with workers from Poland and France. His sister, Eva-Brigitte, was pregnant with her second child. Her husband, Heinz, also a pilot though he was a bomber not a fighter, arranged to be home at the same time as Joachim. Konrad, Joachim's godson, was now a year old and he would be joined by a younger sibling in March.

In Germany, Joachim could see that the war, which Hitler had long expected to be short-lived was taking its toll on the home front. Anti-aircraft batteries were manned by Hitler Youth as young as fifteen and with supplies from Africa cut off, food was more scarce; restaurants were shuttered and there was a ban on nightlife, which the regime deemed unseemly during a time of total war. On January 27, the United States Eighth Air Force sent sixty-four bombers from its base in Britain on its first bombing raid against warehouses and factories at Wilhelmshaven on the North Sea. Joachim learned that American pilots shot down twenty-two German aircraft; total American losses: three.

Not only bombs were reaching Germany; hundreds of thousands of Allied propaganda leaflets also rained from the sky: Words of advice from their British enemies covered the streets to be quickly shoved into a pocket and read in private; the potent conditioning of the last years ran deep and a citizen must not be seen reading the words of the enemy. But they did read them, and particularly in German-occupied territories, partisan activity, long suppressed by terror, grew in strength and frequency. One long British editorial dropped from the sky ends:

You have no chance. You could not defeat us in 1940, when we were almost unarmed and stood alone. Your leaders were crazy to attack Russia as well as America (but then your leaders are crazy; the whole world thinks so except Italy).

How can you hope to win now that we are getting even stronger, having both Russia and America as allies, while you are getting more and more exhausted?

Remember this: no matter how far your armies march they can never get to England. They could not get here when we were unarmed. Whatever their victories, you will still have to settle the air war with us and America. You can never win that. But we are doing so already now.

One final thing: it is up to you to end the war and the bombing. You can overthrow the Nazis and make peace. It is not true that we plan a peace of revenge. That is a German propaganda lie. But we shall certainly make it impossible for any German Government to start a total war again. And is not that as necessary in your own interests as in ours?"[71]

Goebbels' propaganda machine would make every effort to squelch the news about bombings in the north, and to dull the impact of the leaflets, but all the propaganda in the world couldn't hide what happened in Stalingrad when on January 31, 1941, Field Marshal von Paulus surrendered. Of the 284,000 German soldiers in Stalingrad, 160,000 had been killed in action; caught in a pincer trap, many more starved or froze to death, including the group that Joachim's father, Paul Müncheberg, had led and left in Gomel to be absorbed by the 24th Tank Division. The frigid fingers of winter layered the ground with ice, paralyzed vehicles, and froze fingers and eyelids. Those unlucky enough to survive the winter, hobbled on frost-bitten feet towards gulags where many would never arrive and most who did would never leave.

Paul escaped the worst of it as General Field Marshall Kluge had appointed him combat commander at Shisdra, six hundred miles north of Stalingrad. Shisdra was, Paul wrote, "a suicide mission as the Russians were threatening us with tanks and we didn't have any tanks on our side."

Joachim certainly knew what was happening in the East and he knew well the bleak situation in North Africa. While in Berlin, he and his former commanding officer and friend, Adolf Galland, met with Hermann Göring to discuss the Luftwaffe's problems.

The meeting included seven leaders, all Ace pilots who collectively had counted hundreds of victories. Four, including Joachim, were fighter pilots and three were bombers. According to Galland's account, Göring typically began meetings with a long-winded sermon, like the letter Joachim had been ordered to read to his men only two months before, but on this day in early 1943, Reichsmarschall Göring did not lecture the men so much as indict them. The Luftwaffe, he ranted, was responsible for all the recent military failures including Stalingrad. He accused them and all the men who reported to them of failing Germany, of failing to have the fighting spirit and failing to believe in the National Socialist ideals of the perfect Aryan race. He accused them of cowardice, which was punishable by execution, and he demanded the names of pilots who shirked their duties.

The men were stunned.

But they were not silent.

Günther Lützow, an Ace pilot who commanded fighter operations in Italy, was the first to commit what would have been a treasonous act in Nazi Germany, he dared to challenge authority. According to Galland's memoir, Lützow shouted at Göring.

> *Your incompetence and living in the old days will not change the facts, Herr Reichsmarschall! Wise men know their limits, but you obviously have not yet received that education. Well, I am here to tell you that the only cowards I can see are the old men in Berlin giving orders, but not taking the risks, and you are the greatest example! If you wish to change our circumstances, I would suggest that you allow those of us who are leaders lead, and stay out of our way!*[2]

Then in a last suicidal burst, Lützow addressed the Reischsmarschall as *Herr Göring*, stripping him publicly of the dignity of his title.

Joachim and the other pilots in the room, were ashen, silent, their jaws tight, fists clenched. They were seasoned, combat-ready warriors, and they had killed many men, but this was a different kind of combat. They had just watched Günther, their colleague and friend, say out loud what they all knew to be true and for this he would certainly die. Unexpectedly, Göring did not dismiss Lützow. He lowered his voice and turned to the senior pilot in the room, Adolf Galland.

Galland took a deep breath; disagreeing with a superior officer was never condoned, but he also knew that Göring had grown weak within Hitler's hierarchy and Galland supported what Lützow had said. The pilots were doing everything they could, but they needed more support; supply lines were stretched, and they weren't getting the fuel, parts, planes or pilots they needed.

The meeting did not progress well. The pilots, Göring stormed, had lied about their victories and were unworthy of wearing the medals that dangled from their necks. Sensing disbelief, he added, these were accusations from Hitler himself.

This was too much for Galland. He had caught Göring in a lie. In his own words:

> *I knew this was a lie because unknown to Göring I had just met with Hitler a few days before, where he actually praised the fighter pilots and was very impressed with their record...*[73]

Göring then accused Galland of falsifying reports and hiding deficiencies from him.

Seething with fury, Galland stood and one by one, he unhooked and unpinned all his medals and threw them on the heavy oak table.

> *I then told him in front of the assembled men that I would not wear those due to my being "unworthy" along with my men, and then something else happened that is not told very often, and I have not seen in any of the books I have read. Trautloft, Müncheberg, and Lützow also took off their medals from around their necks and placed them on the table.*

The four pilots pushed their chairs back and turned to leave the room.

Göring's jowls quivered with rage and the purple veins in his over-sized face bulged as he shouted at the men leaving the room: They had not been dismissed! Lützow shot back: *"Then I would suggest you tell the Führer that his cowards walked out. You can't shoot us all!"*

In the Third Reich, men were court-martialed and executed—sometimes publicly—for lesser crimes and each man who had just made a stand knew it. *Once the door closed behind us, I will tell you that I was sweating heavily, as were Trautloft and Müncheberg. We were all thinking that we had just terminated our careers, if not our lives.*

The response to their stand was anticlimactic. Nothing happened to the pilots who stripped themselves of their medals and nothing changed at the front. Germany did not have the resources to supply what the pilots needed. The medals were returned to the four pilots and the incident forgotten or buried. It was a moment that remained quietly private, known only to the pilots in the room until Galland wrote of it many years later, well after the war was over.

War makes morality complicated. In the German language, even the words betray this contradiction as the word for "fighter" is Jäger (hunter); but pilots are also known as "Ritter der Luft" (knights of the air) a role that requires adhering to a certain moral and social code. There are many stories on both sides of enemy pilots drifting helplessly, easy targets for other pilots, yet allowed to live because shooting a dangling parachutist was not allowed. If there was an honor code, on that day in early 1943, when Joachim removed the medals he had earned by serving the Third Reich, he aligned himself with the men he fought with and not the Führer, to whom he had sworn his allegiance and whose hand he had so recently grasped in his own. His biographer would write that Müncheberg's motto was "Understand that life teaches you that there is more to honor than honors."

TED

Ted had never been the best student in a class or the most able athlete on the field, but he had a solid moral core and a zest for living big; he made friends wherever he went and he had a love of country that went well beyond concerns for himself. He had been with the 52nd Fighter group for several weeks, but he had stayed in the background, hoping that the men who had fought together out of Bone would accept him as an able colleague. On January 3, after a party at the hotel in Biskra, he had a chance to talk with his Commanding Officer, James Coward.

> *Jim (the C.O.) and I were talking alone, our first talk together. He told me when I came into the outfit he wanted to kick me out because of my rank and former job. Windy [Lt. Col. Graham W. West] and Mac [Captain Norman L. McDonald] prevailed on him to keep me and he told me he was glad to have me and I deserved to wear the bars of a captain.*

The 52nd was assigned to protect the bases of the long-range bombers in the area. At Biskra, the men who had fought at Bone were getting much needed rest and the airdrome was mostly quiet, with no enemy fighter action. But nights were occasionally punctuated by what Ted described as "surprisingly accurate" bombing attacks. There was not much to do, and a highlight was when "Four Jills" took their USO tour to small villages in North Africa populated almost exclusively by soldiers. Every man who was free and able made his way to sit in the dust where for a short time they could watch talented young women sing and dance on the flat bed of a big wrecking truck in the midafternoon sun.[74]

Ted flew patrols, reconnaissance missions, sweeps, and escorted P-39's, often electing to fly the difficult and vulnerable "tail-end Charlie" position, normally occupied by a pilot of lesser rank.

The weather is perfect, when it is not too cold or dusty; dry warm days and cool starry nights. Beautiful colored mountains and lovely sunrises. It is paradoxical flying around in the early dawn with my eye on the sunrise colors and another on the lookout for enemy aircraft.

During the long evenings when they weren't flying Ted tried to get a poker game going. "The men were agreeable," he wrote, "but we had trouble getting enough players as many of the good players had been killed." He was flying daily and described one mission from which he nearly did not return.

I think I can accurately, or with a fair degree of accuracy say what a man feels—I almost said "thinks"—he doesn't—just before a sudden crash that writes him off as I experienced it this morning up to the last second (slow rolling off the "deck"). It is a feeling of suspension and extreme excitement mingled with mild anger—the thought was "dammit you killed yourself." No heroics, no fear, no prayer—no time. It might vary with the individual but I believe under similar circumstances the reaction would be the same.

JOACHIM

Joachim was still on home leave when, on February 18, Joseph Goebbels, Hitler's infamous minister of propaganda, addressed a group of invited guests who he called "the politically best-trained audience you can find in Germany." As a recipient of the Knight's Cross with Swords, Joachim would have been a welcome guest in Goebbels' audience, but he opted to remain in Austria to ski. Undoubtedly, while there he became aware of the content of Goebbels' "total war" speech[75], which was widely broadcast; there could be no mistake: every man, woman and child in Germany was at war and all resources in the nation and occupied territories were mobilized for the effort. The speech was designed to offset the devastating news of Stalingrad and to rouse the assembled believers to an ecstasy of enthusiasm for a war that had already claimed so many young lives on the battlefield.

The small, vain Goebbels, with his pinched squirrel-like face and black hair sleek with oil, stood before an audience of thousands, mostly men, on a high white stage flanked by red and black Nazi flags and medal-bedecked men in their uniforms. From his perch Goebbels shouted and gesticulated wildly as he framed the tragedy at Stalingrad as a heroic stand against Bolshevism and reinforced the righteousness of what had, since 1941, been called "a final solution." "We see Jewry as a direct threat to every nation…Jewry is a contagious infection!" The assembled audience rose periodically in unison, hands outstretched in a stiff-armed Nazi salute, voices raised in a resounding "Yes!"

Yes, to the total war! Yes, to the final solution! Yes, to the sacrifices they were called upon to make. The wealthy and the elite would not be spared. Everyone would be called upon to make sacrifices as military exemptions were canceled, and luxury stores and restaurants closed. They were facing a "hard and pitiless war" and they—the assembled audience and every citizen listening on the radio—could do his part. His final words, "Now, people rise up, and let the storm break loose!" were nearly drowned out as the crowd in the Sportspalast stood in unison, arms raised, shouting "Zeig Heil!" before breaking into the national anthem, announcing to the world that Germany would not falter; they would not be shaken even as their cities were pummeled to rubble and littered with leaflets from heaven, they sang.

Germany, Germany above all,
above all else in the world,
When it steadfastly holds together,

offensively and defensively,
with brotherhood.
From the Maas to the Memel,
from the Etsch to the Belt,
Germany, Germany above all,
above all else in the world.

TED

In Algeria, Ted's squadron moved from Biskra to Youks-les-Bains, Algeria, closer to Tunisia and the front and well in range of enemy bombers. They dug in and carved slit trenches between tents, which gave them some protection as they crouched and crawled from tent to tent. During the second week of February the Germans moved in to vanquish the ill-positioned Allied troops. Rommel sensed the Allies' weakness at Kasserine Pass, which was two hundred miles inland from the port of Tunis. He planned his attack for the part of the chain manned by the inexperienced Americans, which he judged would be the soft spot. The British, too, had failed to reconnoiter the landscape and had relied on maps with inadequate detail. Too late they found out that the pins they had so neatly placed in the maps on the wall did not correspond to the contour of the terrain, and men who were sent to support one another were separated by impassable chasms.

On February 18, as Goebbels shouted his "total war" speech in Berlin, the Allies were taking a pounding at Kasserine Pass and the 52nd squadron was providing escort support for bombers Ted wrote, "*Pack up, we leave in half an hour.*" *We left for the front escorting the transports carrying our equipment. I was in Jim's flight, #3. Warren and Adams also. Jim's engine quit, he had to crash land. Warren and Adams finally found their way back to Biskra and I went on to our destination [Youks-les-Bains].*

On one mission, there was heavy ground fire; many P-39's and one pilot were lost. Ted was flying with the pilot who went down:

We hit a pot full of flack. Roger Newberry got hit, turned on his back and crashed hard. Roddy was the studious type, more adapted to teaching aerodynamics at Randolph Field than flying P-shooters. He was quiet, retiring, and quite nervous. Just before we left Biskra he hit a Grand Slam and stood up and shouted "whoopee" the most noise I ever heard him make... He was engaged and looking forward to his post-war job waiting for him. God bless you, Roddy, we'll miss you!

With the Kasserine Pass fiasco in full swing, the 52nd spent two days at Thélepte, just fifteen miles from the enemy lines. During their short stay, Ted flew a number of missions escorting P-20's and P-39 bombers. For three days they lived in dry river beds and Ted's commanding officer, Norman L. MacDonald who everyone called "Mac," noted that *"because of intermittent artillery fire from the Germans, we slept in shallow holes dug in the ground and in man-made caves. We even took refuge in a small French Foreign Legion chapel one night."*

In his diary, Ted added that the whole squadron found a place to sleep in the church, but Mac had the best spot: the altar. After the church, the men moved by one's and two's into holes in the ground.

Mac and I found a dug-out to live in made by men there before us. It was very comfortable, a stove and bunks. They even left us some real coffee! It was three-quarters underground covered with reeds and dirt. The next morning at 3:30 they got us up and told us to pack immediately as we were evacuating in front of the Germans. I regretted leaving that spot more than any place I've been. We packed and sat in Operations and listened to the German artillery pound near us and watched the fires of our burning gas dumps. We had a backup phonograph which we played to pass the time till daylight huddled underground.

Mac asked the name of a piece they were playing; it was "Celery Stalks at Midnight." He laconically remarked "that's a new name for the bastards."

We took off after dawn and flew sweeps. Troops, trucks and equipment streamed past us, a disheartening sight.

Ordered to burn any planes they couldn't fly out to keep them out of enemy hands, twenty-two charred hulks were left on the field, but all of the thirteen

Spitfires had pilots and could be flown out. Neither Ted nor Mac nor any of the men on the ground could have known how bad it had been at the Kasserine Pass, the first major engagement between American and German troops. They knew the Americans had been beaten, but they didn't know how badly. In ten days, American forces were hurled back fifty miles, lost 183 tanks and more than 3000 men.[76] The 1st Armored Division alone lost 98 tanks, 57 halftracks, 29 artillery pieces and among the five hundred men of the first who died in the muddy outcropping of the pass, was every one of the division's most highly trained tank crews.

Kasserine Pass was a resounding defeat for the Allies, but uncharacteristically Rommel failed to press his advantage, and gave the Americans time to regroup and learn the harsh lessons of defeat. The US General Lloyd Fredendall has been largely criticized for failing to go to the front himself, while micromanaging the men who were there. Too late to make a difference, strategists who later reviewed Fredendall's plan realized that defeat was inevitable. After Kasserine, the Allies were down, but they were not out. US General Ernest Harmon replaced Fredendall and on February 22, despite heavy losses in earlier battles, the US II Corps and British reserves launched a massive offensive, halting the German advance.

Exhausted, ill, disillusioned, and perhaps sensing the catastrophe North Africa would soon become, Rommel ordered his forces east to the coast where the German eagle still buried its talons in a few well-defended coastal positions.

At Youks-les-Bains in Algeria, late wet winter cold was seeping into the American soldiers' bones. Ted and his comrades, yearning for warmth, *built a big fire in our tent (Jerry, Mac, Lynn, Fireball and me) and burned the darned tent down. ….*

JOACHIM

On March 7, two weeks after the United States' first major defeat of the war at Kasserine Pass, Joachim returned to action in North Africa and resumed command of JG 77, which had moved to La Fauconnerie in Tunisia, 160 miles south of the capital city, Tunis. During Joachim's home-leave, the Allies had slowly, fitfully, and at great cost in lives and equipment on both sides reduced the Axis bridgehead in Tunisia.

While Axis resources were sorely stretched, the loss of El Alamein several months earlier, had sharpened Hitler's focus and he sent massive reinforcements to the region. JG 77 had been outfitted with the newest design of the Bf 109 fighter and though it required somewhat different handling, Joachim wrote that the changeover was justified, since he was facing many more P-40's and the newer planes were equipped with heavier armament and better radios.

Even with better equipment, Joachim was well aware of their deficiencies. As he and the other pilots had said to Göring, they did not have either the manpower or the equipment to prevail. The previous summer he had written that "numerically speaking, the opponent is still superior to us three times over!" In the intervening months, the situation had grown far worse as the Allied presence grew exponentially.

He had had a long and welcome break in Germany and Austria, but once in Africa, Joachim was ready again for action and returned immediately to the air. On March 10 he claimed two P-40's shot down in quick succession just north of Kasserine Pass, bringing his victory tally to 131 confirmed kills.

TED

Ted continued to escort bombers and on one mission he followed several 109s and found the German base camp.

> *Vincent got damaged. Sandy and I left the flight to shoot up a B-25 that had crash landed in Jerry country. There was a man running from the scene of the ship. I shot at him with only my 30's and killed him. In two passes I had set the B-25 on fire. Back to the formation and home. We had found their airdrome, which had until now been concealed.*

Ted does not describe the man he killed; it isn't known if his target was in uniform or not. He does identify the aircraft: a B-25, which is a North American built bomber and presumably he shot it up so it could not yield any secrets to the enemy. While there is nothing whatever chivalrous or perhaps even moral about killing a man running for his life away from the scene of a crash, Ted seems proud of what he did, but it was not confirmed, and he doesn't explain it. Still, what he describes as his first kill seems to be a baptism for him.

Perhaps he wanted revenge for Roddy. There is something disturbing in this cold report recorded in his diary. Somewhere along the line, Ted had hardened. He was no longer a young man writing a humorous column for his college newspaper, he had become part of a larger group and they owed their survival to one another. At the same time, he does not seem to hate the Germans as a group. On March 14, he wrote several letters home and a diary entry:

> *Yesterday at noon the 109s strafed our field. I was washing my mess kit and nearly got pushed into the tub when the shooting began. A Spit went after four of them, right into the middle of the formation not knowing two were immediately behind him and they didn't see him. The ack-ack [anti-aircraft gunfire] shot one down in front of us, the pilot pulled up and bailed out from about 400 feet. He was burned a little. He was a Sergeant with the iron cross and 126 sorties, shot down in the channel once before. Spoke French and English. A smart, interesting guy I figured him for.*

The captured pilot was younger than Joachim, but he no doubt knew the commander of the Red Hearts. One of Ted's buddies retold the story of the talkative German pilot:

> *"The young pilot was blue-eyed blond and very talky…. He asked if we were all pilots, and we said that we were—and that there were many, many more on the way. He said, 'Bring them on; we can handle all that you produce!' I think sometimes, that he was about right."* [77]

JOACHIM

Though he did not record any victories on March 13, Joachim may have been among the Messerschmitt's that strafed the field where Ted and the 52nd were stationed that day. For the next few days, weather was poor, hindering activities on both sides, but by March 21, the British 8th Army began large scale attacks along the Mareth line, fortifications originally built to defend Tunisia from attacks by Fascist Libya. In 1943, the Mareth Line was used by the Germans to defend against the British 8th Army. In the fray to hold the line on March 22, Joachim scored his 134th victory, a P-40 flown by Flight Sergeant Maloney, but most of the news that day was not good. The Red Hearts had lost four pilots and they had been unable to stop the Allies from bombing the long columns of trucks loaded with supplies that the Axis forces desperately needed.

TED
On March 22, Ted wrote:

> *This morning we were up at 5 am for a dawn fighter sweep well behind the Jerry's lines. The ceiling over the field was unlimited but east was a solid cloud bank which we climbed over. Just as we got to the top of the overcast the sun was coming up, tinting the cottony topped blanket beneath us. The air was fresh and clean and the sky a crystal blue. Odd how on a mission of death we saw such beauty. War had made beauty visible.*

Later, Ted noted:

> *...the 39's went back with the 31st group as cover. The whole Luftwaffe was waiting for them, 109's, 190's – the sky just full of them. Six of the 39's failed to return; one crashed in flames with pilot. Two of the 31st didn't come back. They failed to do their job.*

As Ernie Pyle wrote, death happened to the other fellow, but never to him. A man has to think that or he'd go crazy.

JOACHIM
Joachim may have thought he, too, would live through the war. For three and a half years, he had flown from edge to edge of the vast conflict. He was one

of the most successful pilots on the western front, and he matched that success on the Russian front and North Africa. When he told his men in November of 1942, *"We will not leave this place,"* it was perhaps not a prescient prognostication of individual destinies so much as it was an articulation of a certainty: Hitler did not countenance retreat.

———

At dawn on March 23, the sun climbed to the edge of the Tunisian desert and melted the cold of the night, limning the horizon with a ragged chain that glowed orange then apricot, then pink. Not a single cloud cast a shadow on the desert landscape that rippled and stretched like scar tissue. For Ted, now in Tunisia at Thélepte, life was hard. Desert winds seasoned every meal with African dust and tents pinned to the hard-packed soil regularly blew up in the night, but the pilots of the 52nd Group were in good spirits. They had been able to fly many missions and were beginning to outnumber enemy planes in the air. Their victories were adding up. The day before, they reached a new daily high, calling eighteen hits on the enemy, nine of which were destroyed. The remainder were labeled "probable" or "damaged."

On the morning of March 23, twelve Spitfires from the 5th Squadron were called to fly, but as they were short pilots and planes they were joined by others, including Ted Sweetland, from the 2nd Squadron. At 0915, all twelve Spitfires took off from Thélepte, flying in a British Box Formation, three columns of four planes. Each of the columns flew close side by side, just 100 feet apart, each whirring propeller fifty feet behind the tail of the plane it followed.

At 0930 on March 23, Major Müncheberg took to the air from La Fauconnerie airfield in Tunisia and headed west accompanied only by his wingman, Lieutenant Strasen. The two Messerschmitt 109's were ten to fifteen thousand feet above the ground on a "free hunt" and reconnaissance mission in the Sened-El Guettar region when they spotted a British Box formation far below them.

Ted was flying in the far right corner of the box, the vulnerable "tail-end Charlie" position he insisted on flying, despite his rank. His section was led by his friend and commanding officer, Norm ("Mac") McDonald. Mac and Ted had been friends since the spring of '42 when they flew together and "raised a little hell," as Mac later put it. In North Carolina they had spent many hours together practicing maneuvers in which they broke to the right, an unconventional move against the torque of the propeller. They thought making such an abrupt turn in an unexpected direction might save them some day.

According to McDonald's combat report, the twelve Allied planes were flying low that clear March morning, at just a thousand to two thousand feet, traveling east on a reconnaissance mission of Sened-Maknassy. They were well into enemy territory when the squadron commander called a ninety-degree left turn, placing the sun behind them, blinding them from the back. [78]

From above and behind, Joachim saw that, while he and his wingman were greatly outnumbered, they had the advantage of altitude and as the Spitfires' box made a precision turn to the left, they knew, too, they had surprise. If the Allied pilots had seen them, they would have scattered, perhaps attacked. Yet there they were: 10,000 feet below, twelve enemy planes in a perfect box, tip to tail, wing to wing.

Joachim singled out his victim and dove for the kill.

Here, in the sharp clear air on a cloudless day, somewhere southwest of Maknassy the storyline frays like a rope, splitting ends that twist in the wind. In combat there are no objective observers and there is no single point of view that can claim the truth. There are only men who report what they believe they saw amidst the speed and tension of a dogfight two thousand feet above the unforgiving earth. [79]

Joachim led the attack. Diving out of the sun, he opened fire and scored a direct hit. Someone, perhaps Ted, yelled "Break!" Strapped inside the tiny cockpit, wearing the red socks his mother had knit for him, Ted could see that his Spitfire was pouring smoke. Lieutenant Strasen, Joachim's wingman, reported that the pilot of the Spitfire probably did not know he was under attack until his machine was "covered with fire."

Having sped in for the kill, Joachim was above and close behind. Too close. Ted's plane was disintegrating, pouring itself into its own slipstream. The American pilots who knew him speculated that Ted knew he was mortally wounded. Maybe Ted was aware that this, his tenth combat mission, would be his last and it needed to count for something; he needed to do his job.

All we can know is that as Joachim bore down, Ted broke hard right.

For that split second, Joachim may have realized his mistake. On his 500th sortie he had closed too close. As their planes collided, Joachim and Ted may have seen each other for the first time, a fleeting glimpse through the cages of their cockpits: near mirrors, young men who had become warriors. Perhaps they both felt what Ted had described in his journal the day he nearly died: *that feeling of suspension and extreme excitement mingled with mild anger...No heroics, no fear, no prayer, no time.*

Exactly what happened in the air that day we can never know, but one truth is irrefutable. At 0950 on the morning of Tuesday, March 23, 1943, two twenty-four-year-old men, born six months and a world apart, crashed. Both men fell to their deaths, etching the earth with the charred wreckage of their planes. From the air, they looked like twin crosses, side by side.

After 500 sorties, Joachim Müncheberg's kill scorecard was closed.

Ted Sweetland was his 135th victory.

Joachim Müncheberg was Ted Sweetland's first.

EPILOGUE

———

I HAD SET OUT TO find out about the man who killed my uncle and I found a boy who came of age in Nazi Germany. Maybe all anyone finds when they scratch below the surface of a warrior is a person willing to fight for what he has been raised to believe.

In Germany I found that how people talk about World War II depends on their personality, their experience and their generation. Those who were alive and old enough to bear some responsibility for the war are a part of the "Tatergeneration," the first or perpetrator generation and they are nearly gone now. Their children, like Konrad and Christian Hoffstätter-Müncheberg, are the "zweite" (second) generation. As yet unborn when the war started, or too young to make decisions on their own, the zweite generation cannot be responsible for the war in which their parents, uncles, and aunts fought and died and yet they, and we, are connected to our histories – with pride or with shame.

The end of the war in Germany in 1945 was ragged, but against all odds, Joachim's sister, Eva, had lived. Before the war was over, she had three children and was living at Friedrichshof with her mother, Erika. Her fourth child, Christian was not born until after the war and he was the one I traced through the phone directories, so I met with him first. He had Joachim's personal photo album and we spent hours poring over it. Then I traveled to Hamburg to meet his oldest brother, Konrad, born in 1942, the eldest of Eva's four children; Joachim had held him in his arms on the day he was christened. Konrad and I sat in a bright corner of a hotel in Hamburg. It's a beautiful city again, rebuilt after it was bombed to rubble in the summer of 1943. Thousands of people died in those bombing raids—many of them civilians, innocent of all except the complicity of silence.

With the big picture window behind him and the clouds scudding across the sky, racing into dark battalions that would bring rain in the afternoon, Konrad told me what he could remember and what his siblings had remembered. When there was no more to tell about Joachim, I asked him about his mother and his grandmother.

It was easy for him to talk about his mother, Eva-Brigitte, who was, he said, much more than a mother—she was a household manager, and a teacher and a very strong woman. She did not talk about Joachim, though Konrad knew that she had loved her brother deeply and missed him. She named his younger brother, Jochen, who was born in the autumn of 1944, after him. But about Joachim's mother, Erika, Konrad was more reticent.

My grandmother was always old, he said, smiling. People aged more then.

Your grandmother's life was not easy, I said.

No, it wasn't.

We were quiet for a long time.

I did not want to press, but I wanted to ask: Did he know how his mother and grandmother had managed to get out of Pomerania? With three babies? I knew the path the Russians had taken as they marched towards Berlin in 1945. I knew a German of any age was vulnerable—particularly a woman. I knew that long after the bombs had stopped, army uniform buttons, artillery shells and shards of shrapnel still emerged when the fields were tilled in spring. I knew that if there had been Germans at Friedrichshof, they would not have been spared the wrath of the Russians who marched across the land seventy years to the day before I was there.

I told Konrad that when I began my search for living relatives of Joachim, I had not had much hope – and yet, here we were. We were sitting in deep leather couches in Hamburg because Joachim's only sister had survived to have three children during the war and a fourth, Christian, several years after the war was over. I told him that I thought Christian must have been a prayer.

Konrad turned to the briefcase he had placed on the leather couch next to him. The hard case was well used and too big for its contents: a few pens lined up in a neat row, a German-English dictionary, and a lone document, 92 pages, typed on thin paper, single-spaced, and dated in crabbed script on the first page: "Winter 1961/62."

He had no memories of those days himself, but after his grandmother, Erika, died his grandfather, Paul, had written a memoir. Later he sent me the whole manuscript, but there in the hotel lobby with my laptop perched on my knees, I recorded the story of their flight in his words. Sometimes he would pause, seeking the English word. In the end, we were both quiet; I because I am a woman, a daughter, and a mother; he because he was talking about his mother and grandmother. He was telling me parts of the story that no one wants to know or talk about, or remember.

It was February, 1945. We were at Friedrichshof – my mother and my sister, Brigitte, who was born five days after Joachim fell. My youngest brother, Jochen, was only a few months old and he had just been baptized. I was three. My mother was twenty-seven years old, with three babies. The Russian guns were near and my grandfather wrote, "the streets of Pomerania were filled with more and more refugees from East and West Prussia; Russian terror as they knew it in WWI sat in their limbs."

I don't know if my mother knew where my father was or even if she knew that he was alive, but one day Theo Lindemann, who had been Joachim's adjutant, landed near Friedrichshof. He was bringing a wounded pilot to the hospital. He told my mother to pack only what was necessary; he would come back for us. Then we flew west—away from the Russians.

A day after my mother left with the three of us in the plane, my grandfather Paul went to the bank in Falkenburg and took his money out! The Russians were maybe just 5 km away, but he was able to get 10,000 RM out of the bank! While he was there, he saw the commanding general who told him that by the time he got back to Friedrichshof, there would be German soldiers setting up quarters in his house – the residents had to leave. The front was on his father's old property at Schönfeld, which was already burned, as was the train station at Virchow. Artillery fire was heavy.

Erika and Paul had packed two trucks full of food, enough for us for about a year, then valuables, carpets, furniture, sufficient fuel... Paul had been discharged in 1944, but he wore his uniform. Private cars were not allowed on the autobahn and the only bridge out was controlled by the German army, but wearing his old uniform my grandfather out-ranked the captain at the bridge, so the captain saluted and let him go. ...

Eva's husband, Heinz, had been captured and sent to a POW camp in Russia and except for Heinz, the rest of the family had gotten to safety—by air and then by road. They were able to stay with friends near Stilow in the north not far from the Baltic Sea, though they were still in Germany. After the war ended and the Allies divided Germany, the northern territory was given to the Russians. When they discovered that Paul had in his possession two guns, he was sent as a POW to Finland. The two women were alone again with three babies.

After nearly five years as a prisoner of war, Paul was released on January 2, 1950. He was nearly seventy years old. In Berlin, he was interviewed by a British Major and about that encounter he wrote:

Then a British major took me into his office, he wanted to know more about my captivity, the Russian relations, factory camps, military institutions that I had perhaps observed. Unfortunately, I could not tell him much since I had not worked anywhere and had not entered a factory. We also talked about our personal experiences in the war. He suddenly said, it must be a depressing, dishonoring feeling as a German officer who had fought in two wars and was defeated.

I asked him to turn around; there was a large world map, covering the whole wall, hanging behind him; Germany was about as big as a hand on the map. I indicated the small Germany; this Germany had had 52 opponents in 1914 who needed four years to bring Germany to its knees, not by military victories on the battlefield but by the starvation of the German population; then 25 years later, the whole world needed five years in order to conquer us. He should look at the map again, at where the front was during the almost nine years of war, the battles were fought on German soil only in the last quarter year!

And we German soldiers shouldn't be proud of our military accomplishments? At any rate, I am proud to have served the brave German people as an officer. Could he, a British officer, have the same feeling? The British people placed so much emphasis on fairness, was it really fair when it, with nearly fifty others, pounced on one country? And then still be proud to have defeated it after five years? If any people can be proud of their accomplishments in these wars, then it was the Germans! The major was silent and somewhat abashed, shook my hand amicably and released me.

For a while after telling me about his grandfather, who remained unrepentant, Konrad was silent, but it seemed he had more to say, so I waited. Behind him a mist of droplets began to spatter the window. Finally, he cleared his throat and began talking again, as if to himself, in rapid German. He was thumbing through his dictionary—brown and worn, finally he said aloud to me:

I do not know this word in English.

I brought up Google Translate. "Spell it," I said. Letter by letter, I typed it in to the box on the left. Then all at once, the translation appeared in the box on the right.

"Rape," it said. "Vergewaltigung means rape."

Yes, he nodded. Then looked at the floor and around the warm lobby of the hotel.

I imagine my mother was raped. My grandmother too. But they never told about it. I never heard a word. I think my mother would never tell my father...I think so...Also, Erika to Paul. I don't think they ever told their husbands what happened.

I needed to cry, but tears felt foolish. There was too much to cry about. Too many victims. Some innocent, some not. Every one of them someone's child, even if they crash to earth or wash ashore and nothing remains to identify them.

Joachim's mother, Erika Müncheberg, died in 1961, a few weeks after traveling to Tunisia to see her son's grave. Paul wrote: *She apparently became indifferent to everything after we visited Achim's grave; nothing seemed to interest her; only flying gave her noticeable joy.* At her service, Psalm 4, Verse 9 was read:
In peace I will lie down and fall asleep, for you alone, Lord, make me secure.

NELL

Nell was alone in the big stone house when two soldiers came to the door bearing a telegram:

The secretary of war desires me to express his deep regret that your son Captain Theodore R. Sweetland was killed in action in defense of his country in North African Area March 23. Letter follows.

Bent by grief that could not be lifted, she went to her room. Nell lived another thirteen years, but she never left the United States again. In her pocket, she always carried the rosary beads she had bought in Rome on Ted's nineteenth birthday. It had been such a joyful occasion. She had given him a medal of Jesus' sacred heart; it was gold and thick but also delicate. She hoped he had been wearing it close to his own heart on that blue sky day, his last on earth.

On that day, she had been writing letters at the little knob-legged desk in her room, admonishing Jack to write to his brother, "who is in there pitching," though afterwards she knew that by the time she wrote those words, Ted was already dead.

Six of Nell's children lived on and there was life still to be cherished, marriages to celebrate, grandchildren born, and though she never talked about Ted, she never stopped grieving him. My father, Eugene, could not talk about his older brother—even decades later. When we asked, he would choke a little, and clear his throat, but his eyes would tear and then he would shake his head. His brother died ten days before his nineteenth birthday; they had traveled together in Europe in 1938; he idolized him, but that's all we knew. My dad had two sons before he named the third Theodore Reilly Sweetland II. My brother, also known as Ted, was born in 1960.

———

As I followed the skein of my brother's namesake, I was never far from thinking about his parents' grief, which never found a voice. Nor were Joachim's parents able to articulate their sorrow. In his memoir, Paul records the logistics of what happened on the day his son died, but about his feelings, he remained silent:

> On March 23, 1943, I was sitting with my men playing Doppelkopf[80] when I was called to the telephone at 10 pm; it was the military personnel office in Berlin: Achim had fallen just before 10 that morning in Tunisia during his 135th air victory. General von Scheele was already with me early the next day, also I received condolences from General Field Marshal von Kluge; they offered me immediate leave; I gave each of my positions to a representative and went to the train tracks where the field marshal had ordered a railcar for me. A flight captain was waiting for me in Briansk who flew me to Smolensk. I had to overnight there with my men since my plane had to take a severely wounded general to Berlin. I should have been brought to von Kluge's headquarters to sleep but requested to be allowed to sleep in the soldier's home since I wasn't in the mood for conversation; permission granted; I was woken at 4 am the next day and brought to a courier train with only 2 first class cars to Berlin. I would rather remain silent about the following difficult days in Friedrichshof. There was one bright spot – the birth of Brigitte on March 28; the women then had an earnest diversion.

At the beginning of my journey to find Joachim, I traveled from Berlin across Germany before I met Christian. I stopped in Cologne and meandered the back streets, looking for the shell of a church that holds Käthe Kollwitz's sculpture, *Parents*.

One of Germany's most important twentieth century artists, Kollwitz believed that art could promote social change; themes of poverty and war, grief and death dominate her work, which was banned by the Nazis. On a small side street, several blocks from the cathedral that towers over the city, I found her sculpture of *Parents* who are kneeling, immobile, forever grieving, as she was for her own son who died in WWI. Iron bars separated me from the man and the woman who share a space within the shattered walls of the church. They are together, but separate, too far apart to be touched or consoled, each grieving in their own way. He looks stoic, hugging himself, but perhaps he's only trying desperately to hold himself together. She is angled towards him, stooped as if burdened by an invisible weight. The space between them is empty, an echo of the son they lost.

I walked slowly back to the cathedral, lingering for coffee, leaning back in my white plastic chair on the sidewalk to take in the gothic spires reaching like clasped hands to the heavens painted that day a steely blue feathered with clouds. Inside the cathedral it was dark and a little cold on that warm spring day, but its massive, Gothic weight somehow eased my heart. The building was begun in the thirteenth century and completed in the nineteenth by the faithful, adhering to the original medieval plans.

As the war wound to its end, which had long been inevitable, the city was bombed, and when the bombs stopped, the cathedral was one of the few buildings that remained standing. At noon on that spring day, the choir began to sing, their voices rose, echoing against the high Gothic dome, and for me, the vast interior space filled with the spirits of those who died in that long ago war and the prayers of their parents who outlived them.

The day after Joachim died, the Allies bombed La Fauconnerie, the German airfield where the Red Heart squadron was stationed. Joachim's long-haired dachshund, Seppl, who had been with him at every base on every front, died in the attack. Forty-four days later, on May 7, 1943, the Afrika Korps surrendered, giving the Allies the bases they needed to liberate Europe from the grasp of a man named Adolf Hitler.

Joachim Müncheberg with his dog, Seppl

Ted Sweetland

ACKNOWLEDGEMENTS

———

THIS BOOK WOULD NOT HAVE been possible if Joachim's nephews, Christian and Konrad Hoffstätter-Müncheberg, had not shared Joachim's personal photo album, his father's memoir, and many family stories that gave life to this manuscript. On the American side, many thanks to Theodore Reilly Sweetland II; Sandra Poole Sweetland; Eugene David Sweetland, Jr.; Mary Sweetland Laver; Lance Laver; Anne Sweetland Kirby; Nicholas Sweetland Edwards and Allison Stark Edwards whose belief in and support of this project never wavered. A special thank you to my husband, Lee Edwards, and my daughter, Haley Sweetland Edwards, who read, reread, and read yet again the manuscript, each time providing editorial corrections, historical insights, and another dose of encouragement. I wish there were more ways to say thank you.

I could not have discovered what I did without the help of my intrepid researchers, translators and guides: Mara Goldwyn and Hans-Jochen Krank-Hover in Germany; Magda Smolensk of the Poznan Project in Poland; Father Gerald McKevitt, S.J. and Sheila Conway at Santa Clara University; Father Jerry Wade, S.J., and Matthew Zuniga at Bellarmine College Preparatory; Kevin Wallace at the Beatrice Wood Center for the Arts; Kurt Spence and Hap Griffith for insights on the military; Noa Wheeler for early editorial guidance, and Andrea Graves for many pages of translation.

I am grateful, too, for a host of friends whose thoughtful questions and unrelenting encouragement prodded me on and especially to Peggy Tranovich, who enriched my journey of discovery as we traveled across Germany together. I remain ever grateful to my dad, Eugene David Sweetland, whose love for his brother and lifelong interest in the lessons of history continue to inspire me. To my mom, Nancy Seeliger Sweetland, who shared with me her own memories of the war years and her passionate belief that it is we the people who are responsible for what we are teaching our children every day.

Jane Sweetland holds degrees in American studies, counseling, education, and an MFA in creative nonfiction. She has taught history and English and is the author of *Washington Monthly*'s *The Other College Guide.*

BIBLIOGRAPHY

Atkinson, Rick. *An Army at Dawn,* Henry Holt & Co, 2002.

Arendt, Hannah. *Eichmann in Jerusalem: A Report on the Banality of Evil.* Penguin Books, 1963.

Baker, Everett Moore and Herbert Hitchen and Vivian T. Pomeroy, editors. *Think on These Things: Sources of Courage, Hope and Faith for Those Serving their Country.* Association Press, 1943.

Baker, Nicholson. *Human Smoke: The Beginnings of World War II, the End of Civilization.* Simon and Schuster, 2008.

Bungay, Stephen. *The Most Dangerous Enemy: A History of the Battle of Britain.* Aurum Press, 2001.

Bytwerk, Randall. *Bending Spines.* Michigan State U.P., 2004.

Calvin College, German Propaganda Archive. *Speeches and Writings by Nazi Leaders. War Propaganda: 1939-45.* http://research.calvin.edu/german-propaganda-archive

Cooke, Alistair. *The American Home Front: 1941-1942.* Grove Press, 2006.

Evans, Richard. *The Third Reich in History and in Memory.* Oxford U.P., 2015.

EyeWitness to History, "Signing the Treaty of Versailles, 1919," www.eyewitnesstohistory.com (2005).

Fagothey, Austin, S.J., *Right and Reason: Ethics in Theory and Practice Based on the Teachings of Aristotle and St. Thomas Aquinas.* 2nd ed., TAN Books, 2000.

Favreau, Marc, editor. *A People's History of World War II: The Worlds' Most Destructive Conflict, As Told by the People Who Lived Through It.* The New Press, 2011.

Galland, Adolph. *The First and the Last.* Bantam, 1979.

Giacomini, George F., Jr. and Gerald McKevitt, S.J. *Serving the Intellect, Touching the Heart: A Portrait of Santa Clara University 1851-2002.* Santa Clara U. P., 2000.

Gilbert, Martin. *The Second World War: A Complete History.* Henry Holt, 1989.

Gray, J. Glenn. *The Warriors: Reflections on Men in Battle, 2nd ed.,* Harper Torch Books, 1967.

Grunberger, Richard. *Twelve Year Reich: A Social History of the Third Reich.* Phoenix, 2005.

Harwood, Jeremy. *Hitler's War: World War II as portrayed by Signal the International Nazi Propaganda Magazine.* Zenith Press, 2014.

Hauptman, Hermann. *The Rise and Fall of the Luftwaffe.* Fonthill Media, 2012.

Heaton, Colin D. and Anne-Marie Lewis. *The German Aces Speak: World War II Through the Eyes of Four of the Luftwaffe's Most Important Commanders.* Zenith, 2011.

Hedges, Chris. *War is a Force that gives Us Meaning.* Anchor Books, 2002.

Hitler, Adolf. *Mein Kampf.* Trans. Ralph Mannheim. First Mariner Books, 1999.

Ivie, Tom and Ludwig, Paul. *From Spitfires and Yellow Tail Mustangs: The U.S. 52nd Fighter Group in World War II.* Google Books, 2015.

Kallis, Aristotle A. *Nazi Propaganda and the Second World War.* Palgrave Macmillan, 2008.

Kertzer, David I. *The Popes Against the Jews: The Vatican's Role in the Rise of Modern Anti-Semitism.* Alfred A. Knopf, 2001.

Kertzer, David I., *The Pope and Mussolini: The Secret History of Pius XI and the Rise of Fascism in Europe.* Random House, 2014.

Kirby, Dale. *Ernest John Sweetland and his Fifty Years of Inventing.* Dale Kirby, 1993.

Kurowski, Franz. *Luftwaffe Aces: German Combat Pilots of WWII.* Stackpole, 2004.

Kushner, Tony. *A Bright Room Called Day.* Theater Communications Group, 1994.

Luftwaffe Records: *Joachim Müncheberg.* http://www.luftwaffe.cz/muncheberg.html

McCombs, Don and Fred L. Worth, editors. *World War II: 4,139 Strange and Fascinating Facts.* Wings Books, 1983.

McKevitt, S.J., Gerald. *The University of Santa Clara: A History 1851-1977.* Stanford U.P., 1979.

Miller, Webb. *I Found No Peace: The Journal of a Foreign Correspondent.* The Literary Guild, 1936.

Müncheberg, Paul. *A Memoir.* Unpublished, 1962.

Nagorski, Andrew. *Hitlerland: American Eyewitnesses to the Nazi Rise to Power.* Simon and Schuster, 2012.

Nicholson, Sir Harold. "Signing the Treaty of Versailles: 1919." http://www. eyewitnesstohistory.com/versailles.htm

Niemoeller, Martin. *Of Guilt and Hope.* Philosophical Library, 1947.

Pine, Lisa. *Education in Nazi Germany,* Berg, 2010.

Plüschow, Gunther. *The Aviator of Tsingtao: My War in China and Escape.* E-Book. 2015.

Price, Alfred. *Luftwaffe.* Ballantine, 1969.

Pullman, John D. and James J. Van Patten. *History of Education in America* (7th edition). Merrill, 1999.

Pyle, Ernie. *Here is Your War.* Henry Holt and Company, 1943.

Roberts, Andrew. *The Storm of War: A New History of the Second World War.* Harper, 2011.

Röll, Hans-Joachim. *Major Joachim Müncheberg: Vom König der Malta-Jäger zum legendären Jäger-Ass von Tunis.* Flechsig, 2014.

Schumann, Ralf and Wolfgang Westerwelle. *Knight's Cross Profiles, volume 2.* Schiffer Military History, 2013.

Sebald, W.G. *On the Natural History of Destruction.* The Modern Library, 2004.

Shirer, William L. *Berlin Diaries.* Alfred A. Knopf, 1941.

Shirer, William L. *The Rise and Fall of the Third Reich: A History of Nazi Germany*. Simon and Schuster, 1960.

Speer, Albert. *Inside the Third Reich: Memoirs by Albert Speer*. Trans. Richard and Clara Winston. The Macmillan Company, 1970.

Spielvogel, Jackson J. *Hitler and Nazi Germany: A History*. 5th ed., Pearson/ Prentice Hall, 2005.

Stargardt, Richard. *The German War: A Nation Under Arms, 1939-1945: Citizens and Soldiers*. Basic Books, 2015.

Terkel, Studs. *"The Good War": An Oral History of World War II*. Pantheon Books, 1984.

The American Beagle Squadron. *The American Beagle Squadron: A History of the Second Fighter Squadron in World War II*. 2nd ed., The American Beagle Squadron, 2006.

The Caen Memorial. *World War II: The Unseen Visual History*. Trans. Christopher Caines. The New Press, 2011.

Ulrich, Robert. *The Education of Nations: A Comparison in Historical Perspective* (Rev. Ed.) Harvard UP, 1967.

United States Holocaust Memorial Museum. *State of Deception: The Power of Nazi Propaganda*. United States Holocaust Memorial Museum, 2009.

United States War Department. *Instructions for American Servicemen in Britain 1942*. Bodleian Library, U of Oxford, 1994.

Wallace, Kevin. *Every Exit is an entry: The Life and Work of Liam O'Gallagher*. Beatrice Wood Center for the Arts, 2009.

Walsh, Charles J., S.J., "Address of the President of the University." *The Owl*. October, 1940.

Ward, Arthur. *A Guide to War Publications of the First and Second World War: From Training Guides to Propaganda Posters*. Pen and Sword Military, 2014.

Watkin, Lawrence Edward. *On Borrowed Time*. Doubleday, Doran & Company, 1937.

Weinberg Gerhard L. *Germany, Hitler, and World War II*. Cambridge U.P., 1995.

Wick, Steve. *The Long Night: William L. Shirer and the Rise and Fall of the Third Reich*. Palgrave Macmillan, 2011.

Wykes, Alan. *Goebbels*. Ballantine, 1973.

Zeller, Frederic. *When Time Ran Out: Coming of Age in the Third Reich*. The Permanent Press, 1989.

1. This story of Joachim's birth is based on the memories, stories, and traditions of the Müncheberg family as recalled by Joachim's nephews, Konrad and Christian Müncheberg-Hoffstätter and told to the author in May, 2015. Though neither remembered him personally, Konrad is Joachim's godson and was, like his uncle, born in the family home at Friedrichshof. The time of his birth was recorded in his father's memoir.

2. The details of Ted's birth are reconstructed from family stories and from the centennial history of Mountainside Hospital in Montclair, New Jersey.

3. In January 1922, Ernest John Sweetland applied for a US Patent (#1,594,334) for the work he had been doing around the time of Ted's birth. His oil filter for automobiles was the subject of a lawsuit between General Motors and the lone inventor, which after twelve years of litigation was settled in Sweetland's favor.

4. This first person account is from "Signing the Treaty of Versailles, 1919," EyeWitness to History, retrieved from http://www.eyewitnesstohistory. com/versailles.htm

5. In his biography of Ted's father, Dale Kirby wrote. "By 1903, he [Ernest John Sweetland] was a Mason—and would, in fact, become a 32nd degree Mason years later. At their 4th of July event in Virginia City in 1903, Dad was invited to be an aide to the Grand Marshall." (page 47)

6. This reference is from David Kertzer's Pulitzer prize-winning book, *The Popes Against the Jews*. "In his 1543 essay *On the Jews and Their Lies*, Luther branded the Jews a "plague of disgusting vermin" who sought world domination. He urged that their books, synagogues, schools, and houses be burned." Page 17.

7. In *Berlin Diaries*, William L. Shirer writes that his "…most vivid first impressions of the citizens of the New Germany had to do with the unquestioning loyalty with which many of them supported the Nazis as Hitler rebuilt a formerly defeated, chaotic country. …At first churches heralded the rise of Hitler as the bringer of a restored moral order."

8. Randall Bytwerk cites Elizabeth Noelle-Neumann who labeled the phenomenon the "spiral of silence." Page 137

9. A story in The *American Experience* series tells of Father Coughlin's background and influence, including a note that for a time, he was "the hero of Nazi Germany." Under pressure from clergy and the Roosevelt administration, Father Coughlin lost his bully pulpit in 1939. http://www.pbs.org/wgbh/amex/holocaust/peopleevents/pandeAMEX96.html

10. In his book *The Pope Against the Jews,* David Kertzer explains the difference between anti-Semitism (racial) and anti-Judaism (religious and social) Page 8. In Volume I, Book XI of *Mein Kampf,* Hitler makes clear that he considers all Jews to be racially Jewish, regardless of their faith.

11. In the Berlin Diaries, on September 27, 1937, Shirer wrote: "Much of what is going on and will go on could be learned by the outside world from Mein Kampf, the Bible and Koran together of the Third Reich." Page 85.

12. In his introduction to William L. Shirer's work, *The Rise and Fall of the Third Reich,* Ron Rosenbaum writes: It was the *Post* that discovered and published on December 9, 1931, a secret Nazi Party post-takeover plan for the Jews in which can be found the first known use of the Nazi party euphemism for genocide—"Endlossung," Final Solution. Page xix.

13. The excerpt was written by Ted, though it was for his weekly column after he graduated from high school. His column, "Cabbages and Kings" appeared in the *Santa Clara*, his college newspaper, beginning in January 1939. This column appeared in February 8, 1940.

14. From a speech by Goebbels, January 9, 1928, accessed from Calvin College's German Propaganda Archive. http://research.calvin.edu/german-propaganda-archive/goeb54.htm The archive is curated by Randall L. Bytwerk, author of *Bending Spines,* which provides a deep discussion of Nazi propaganda.

15. In *The Rise and Fall of the Third Reich,* William L. Shirer writes: "There was some ground for this appropriation of Nietzsche as one of the originators of the Nazi Weltanschauung [world view]. Had not the philosopher thundered against democracy and parliaments, preached the will to power, praised war and proclaimed the coming of the master race and the superman—and in the most telling aphorisms? A Nazi could proudly quote him on almost every conceivable subject, and did." Page 100.

16. Lisa Pine supports her scholarly work about *Education in Nazi Germany* with many primary sources including *Hitler's Table Talk* 1941-44: His Private Conversations (Trevor-Roper, 1976), from which this quote is taken. (Page 13.)

17. In his book, *The Education of Nations: A Comparison in Historical Perspective,* Robert Ulrich parses the difference between the practice of indoctrination in democracies and totalitarian systems. First, indoctrination that is truly democratic aims at enhancing the dignity and freedom of the individual within a framework of values believed to be conducive of this end. Totalitarian indoctrination, on the other hand, aims at securing the vassalage of man under a tyrannically construed set of regulations. Second, since such regulated beliefs do not grow organically from the people's tradition, they cannot be taught in a natural dialogue between teacher and pupil but have to be imposed upon both, either by promise of enticing reward, or by threat of severe punishment." Page 211-12

18. Presidential Address by Charles J. Walsh, S.J., to the faculty of Santa Clara University published in *The Owl*, October 1940.

19. Robert Ulrich. Pages 211-212.

20. Franz von Papen's quote is cited from the History Place: The Rise of Adolf Hitler. http://www.historyplace.com/worldwar2/riseofhitler/named.htm

21. The loss of individuals' right to privacy during the Nazi era is detailed in many of the books used as reference. For an overview online, the US Holocaust Museum website: https://www.ushmm.org/outreach/en/article.php?ModuleId=10007673

22. In a web exhibit sponsored by the University of Arizona Library, the official speech by Joseph Goebbels on the night of May 10, 1933, as reported by the official Nazi newspaper is translated. The cite indicates that despite "official" German reporting, the burnings were not a spontaneous act on the part of the German Students Association. http://www.library.arizona.edu/exhibits/burnedbooks/goebbels.htm

23. As Lisa Pine writes, while Christianity was not outlawed, Nazi education usurped the roles of church and family, through tightly regimented educational practices and youth groups. "Religious symbols and images such as crucifixes were banned from schools." Page 29.

24. Inauguration speeches were traditionally in March until FDR's second inaugural address, which began the tradition of January speeches. The complete typewritten text of his inaugural address is available through the National Archives at https://www.archives.gov/education/lessons/fdr-inaugural

25. A detailed account of the Night of the Long Knives is available at the History Place http://www.historyplace.com/worldwar2/timeline/roehm.htm

26. An undated document, The Characteristics of Jesuit Education was accessed at the website of The Jesuit Curia in Rome. http://www.sjweb.info/documents/education/characteristics_en.pdf

27. William Shirer's description of the Nuremburg Rally is from *Berlin Diaries.* Page 21.

28. After Ted died, his friend, William Gallagher, whom he knew as Bill, reverted to the Irish origin of his name, Liam O'Gallagher, and became a successful artist, whose life is documented in a biography by Kevin Wallace, *Every Exit is an Entry.* Liam was the sole beneficiary of Ted's will.

29. The Catholic Journal that supported a boycott of the 1936 Olympics in Nazi Germany was *The Commonweal*, published November 8, 1935.

30. From National Public Radio story by Tom Goldman, *Was Jesse Owens' 1936 Long-Jump Story a Myth?* August 14, 2009. Goldman writes that while the historical record indicates that the story about the German competitor, Luz Long, coaching Jessie Owens in the long jump is apocryphal, the letter he wrote to Owens is true. http://www.npr.org/templates/story/story.php?storyId=111878822

31. From the Santa Clara College year book, The Redwood, 1938.

32. This story of the bombing of Guernica is by Harrison LaRoche from the United Press. It was published on page one in Ted's hometown newspaper, the Oakland Tribune, April 27, 1937, accessed from www.newspapers.com

33. According to Ralph Manheim's English translation of the first edition of Mein Kampf, Hitler likened Jews to egoistic vermin intent on self-preservation. Page 302. The quote about the "Hebrew corrupters" is in the last chapter of the book. Page 679.

34. From The History Place, "Nazis Take Austria," http://www.historyplace.com/worldwar2/triumph/tr-austria.htm,

35. Under a banner "Germany, Austria United, Hitler Tells World; Nazi Soldiers Held "Ready for Any Sacrifice," Ferdinand C.M. Jahn, wrote a

story *Vienna Hails Nazi Soldiers,* Oakland Tribune, March 13, 1938, page 1. Accessed from https://www.newspapers.com/

36. This quote is by Stephen Ambrose, from his book Citizen Soldiers: The U.S. Army from the Normandy Beaches, To the Bulge, To The Surrender of Germany. Converted to the Web and Accessed at World War II History Info: http://www.worldwar2history.info/Army/Jim-Crow.html

37. Charles J. Walsh, S.J., President of Santa Clara College in "A Letter to the Community," *The Owl*, October 1940.

38. BBC diary of a couple of American soldiers on a break from action in Ravello.

39. This quote and the longer citation above it is from, *The Rise and Fall of the Luftwaffe,* written in 1942 and published in 1943 by a pseudonymous "Hauptmann Hermann." Despite the anonymous origin of the work, many details have proved to be true. Page 155.

40. Pope Pius XI died on February 10, 1939, seven months after Ted and his family had an audience with him at his summer home. The editorial, *"Achille Ratti, Pope Pius XI,"* The Santa Clara, February 16, 1939, page 2, was written by Allan Hugh Smith.

41. The full text of Hitler's January 30, 1939, speech before the Reichstag is available through Indiana University Press at https://www.jstor.org

42. Hauptman Hermann, Page 127.

43. According to William Shirer in *The Rise and Fall of the Third Reich*, the only person to openly challenge Hitler was General Thomas, head of the Economics and Armaments branch of the OKW, which directed operations for the German Armed Forces. Thomas argued that "A quick war and a quick peace were a complete illusion. An attack on Poland would

unleash a world war and Germany lacked the raw materials and the food supplies to fight it." Keitel disagreed. Page 518.

44. In Berlin Diaries, Shirer notes that on October 8, 1939, there were a whole page of death notices. Page 233.

45. William L. Shirer, *The Rise and Fall of the Third Reich*, page 669

46. Nicholas Stargardt, *The German War: A Nation Under Arms, 1939-1945*. Page 18.

47. From "Stories of the Battle of Britain—Spitfires Join the Fighting:"In nine days more than 300,000 soldiers were to be evacuated from the only remaining harbor at Dunkirk and the surrounding beaches. Much of the work, especially towards the end of the period was done by "Little Ships of Dunkirk", a hastily but very effectively assembled fleet of civilian merchant and fishing boats, fire ships, paddle steamers, private yachts and motorboats, barges and RNLI lifeboats." http://spitfiresite.com/2010/05/battle-of-britain-1940-spitfires-join-the-fighting.html

48. Arthur D. Levine "was one who manned the boats" at Dunkirk. His account was retrieved from http://www.eyewitnesstohistory.com/dunkirk.htm

49. The transcript of Winston Churchill's speech of June 18, 1940, was accessed from http://www.winstonchurchill.org/resources/speeches/1940-the-finest-hour/122-their-finest-hour

50. The description of the bombing of Berlin is from William L. Shirer, *Berlin Diaries*.

51. The only other foreign recipient of the Italian Gold Medal for bravery was Hans-Joachim Marseille, who became known as the "Star of Africa."

52. In his June 18, 1940 entry in the Berlin Diaries, Shirer wrote: It seems funny, but every German soldier carries a camera…photographing Notre-Dame,

the Arc de Triomphe, the Invalides…Thousands of German soldiers gather all day long at the Tomb of the Unknown Soldier, where the flame still burns under the Arc. They bare their blond heads and stand there gazing… Page 413.

53. Knight's Cross Profiles, page 163.

54. Stephen Bungay, *The Most Dangerous Enemy: A History of the Battle of Britain.*

55. Knight's Cross Profiles, page 166.

56. Knight's Cross Profiles, page 170.

57. This story is as reported by Hans-Joachim Röll in his biography of Joachim and translated for the author by Andrea Graves.

58. In *Hitler's War*, Jeremy Harwood reports that these statements by Hitler and Goebbels were made to Walter Hewel, a foreign liaison officer. Page 132.

59. Statistics about aircraft losses were retrieved from the World War II Foundation http://www.wwiifoundation.org/students/wwii-aircraft-facts/

60. The description of Eisenhower's office is as reported by Rick Atkinson in his Pulitzer Prize winning book, *An Army at Dawn*. Page 157.

61. Norman L. McDonald (O 430835); John F. Pope (O 415348); John Aitken, Jr. (438002) were all members of the "American Beagle Squadron" who survived the war.

62. In his biography of Joachim, Hans Röll cites the journal of Armin Köhler, in the book "Aerial Battle between Sand and Sun" (Luftkampf zwischen Sand und Sonne) by Hans Ring and Christopher Shores as the source of the response to Göring's message.

63. Diary entry is as reported by Ralf Schumann in his biography of Joachim and other Aces in his book *Knight's Cross Profiles.* Page 179

64. Eisenhower's Thanksgiving menu is from *The Army at Dawn*, page 194; Ted's is from his diary.

65. Like the Messerschmitt and the British Spitfire, FW190's are a German single-seat, single-engine fighter aircraft.

66. From Rick Atkinson's Pulitzer-prize winning book, *An Army at Dawn*, a deeply reported story of what happened in North Africa during Operation Torch. Page 184.

67. Censorship was widespread and included personal letters, *An Army at Dawn*, page 196. Ted's letters from England and North Africa are each stamped "censored" by TR Sweetland.

68. Ernie Pyle, *Here is Your War,* page 102.

69. *An Army at Dawn*, page 198

70. Hans-Joachim Röll, page 124.

71. This leaflet is credited to the Marshal of the Royal Air Force, Sir Arthur Harris. Complete transcript accessed at https://jrbenjamin. com/2014/05/21/your-leaders-are-crazy-the-leaflet-we-dropped-on-nazi-germany/ The citation on the site is to Arthur Ward's *Guide to War Publications of the First & Second World War,* a rich source of propaganda used on both sides.

72. Galland's report is recorded in Colin D. Heaton and Anne-Marie Lewis's reporting about Adolf Galland, the "General of the Fighters," in *The German Aces Speak*. Page 108.

73. Ibid., page 109.

74. *Here is Your War.* Page 61.

75. Goebbels' speech, "Nation, Rise Up, and Let the Storm Break Loose," was accessed through Calvin College http://research.calvin.edu/german-propaganda-archive/goeb36.htm

76. Stephen Budiansky, a former national security correspondent, has written extensively on military history and foreign affairs. This descriptive excerpt is from his article "Triumph at Kasserine Pass" accessed online at http://www.historynet.com/triumph-at-kasserine-pass.htm

77. Recollection of Miles R. Lynn, as recorded in *The American Beagle Squadron, page 61.*

78. The battle is described by several American witnesses who were in the air that day and published in *The American Beagle Squadron.*

79. In *The American Beagle Squadron,* Norm MacDonald wrote, "Sweetie was an excellent pilot, but had trouble in the beginning because he was a left-hander all the way. Nevertheless, he really could handle a fighter plane. Back in the States, in P-40s, he and I and Jerry Simpson used to practice all our maneuvers to the right. We would do turns, rolls, including the roll at the top of the Immelmann turn, to the right. We thought that these unconventional maneuvers, opposite to the easier engine torque assisted turns and rolls to the left might be a life saver some day. I'm sure they were for me, but in this particular encounter they may have cost Sweetie his."

Several contradictory accounts of this air battle are recorded by both the Germans and the Americans. On the German side, there are reports that Joachim survived the crash, and died shortly after on the ground. His nephew refutes this account. Joachim's wingman "was forced to conclude that Joachim's machine went through the dregs of the disintegrating Spit, critically damaging his plane, giving Joachim no chance to bail out."

American pilot, Ralph "Gene" Keyes, wrote that Ted "turned sharply upward and to the left, directly into the path of the oncoming ME-109… He saw two flaming spots where the two planes crashed. Both countries report that these two pilots were responsible for the other's death.

80. Doppelkopf is a trick-taking card game.

Made in the USA
Middletown, DE
12 September 2017